SERBIAN INFERNO

Dr. Borko B. Djordjevic, M.D., Ph.D., F.r.c.s.

Serbian Inferno

Published by Quipper Prints
875 North Michigan Avenue,
John Hancock Center,
31st Floor,Chicago, IL 60611
www.quipperprints.com

ISBN (paperback): 978-1-77839-103-3
eISBN: : 978-1-77839-104-0

Contents

THE REVISION OF THE WASHINGTON DECISION

The official visit of Aleksandar Vucic, the President of the Republic of Serbia, to the Serbian people in Kosovo and Metohija in September 2018 was accompanied by Albanian nationalists' shooting from automatic weapons, making death threats, and executing the prohibition of passage. Hashim Thaçi and Ramush Haradinaj, the President and the Prime Minister of the so-called independent Kosovo had attempted to cancel this announced visit of Aleksandar Vucic. Nevertheless, the visit took place because the official Washington warned the authorities of Kosovo that they ought to respect human rights and the political dialogue with Belgrade that they had committed to by signing the Brussels Agreement. The visit of Aleksandar Vucic to Serbian people, to Gazimestan, Kosovska Mitrovica, and other places presented a significant progress in the resolution of the Kosmet issue, but also a signal for taking an initiative in negotiations with Albanian politicians in Pristina.

Aleksandar Vucic in Kosovo and Metohija

At the same time, in Belgrade, a group of old socialists proposed to the Government of Serbia to erect a monument to Slobodan Milosevic, an archon who rose as the national leader at the rally of the Serbs in Kosovo Polje in 1987, but who had thereafter politically lapsed precisely because of betraying the

1

people in Kosovo and Metohija. The proposal of the Socialists, submitted by the honorary president of the SPS (Socialist Party of Serbia) himself, to the City Assembly of Belgrade to erect a bronze statue of Slobodan Milosevic in the capital city of Serbia is the worst thing that could have happened to Serbia, its people, the Government of Serbia, and the President Vucic in the moments of their struggle for the country's integrity and its entry into the European political society.

The idea of erecting a monument to Milosevic is not a new one. Several years ago, it was first suggested by Milutin Mrkonjic, Branko Ruzic, and Momir Bulatovic. And, shortly after that, the president of the Socialists, Ivica Dacic, asserted that his political father, Slobodan, deserved a monument "the same as every other statesman to whom this nation is indebted and for which he fought – and Milosevic did all that".

Milosevic's heirs even proposed several possible locations for his monument in Belgrade –Slavija Square, Academy Park, or Students' Square, next to which the headquarters of SPS are located. The submission of the request to the City Assembly of Belgrade for the erection of a monument to the Serbian archon was hindered by a sudden appointment of Jasmina Mitrovic Maric, the president of the City Commission for Monuments and Names of Streets and Squares, the Ambassador of Serbia in Denmark. Thus, the initiative was delayed for a while.

Bringing Milosevic back into the political life of Serbia, even in the form of a bronze statue, would signify that Serbia is a country of devious politicians. In the previous years, while the state leadership of Serbia have been convincing the international community that we have atoned for the sins of war, that we are dedicated to democracy, that we foster the diplomacy of tolerance and understanding, that we, as a nation, advocate the peace in the Balkans, the public honoring of the man who led us into the war with the western world in the 1990s and who made his nation bleed would mean that we, the Serbs, and politicians, and the whole nation, are again walking with lead boots on our feet.

Borko Djordjevic, MD, a Republican, a Serbian patriot, and a doctor

Slobodan Milosevic came to power in 1986 at the 8th Plenary Session of the Central Committee of the League of Communists of Serbia in a well-organized conspiracy against the liberal wing of the party led by Ivan Stambolic and Dragisa Pavlovic. He brought to power loyal mediocrities, craving for power, money, influence, and authority. He organized a series of "spontaneous" mass rallies damaging institutions and he seized power in provinces.

He committed a coup-d'état in Montenegro and tried to assassinate its President Milo Djukanovic. In 1990, he adopted a constitution in which Serbia de facto seceded from the rest of the SFRY and, thereby, he destroyed the Yugoslav political order.

He was a dogmatic communist and he wished to resemble Josip Broz Tito as a fighter for the preservation of Yugoslavia, but with the ideology of great-Serbia nationalism. During his first stay in Kosmet, when he met the crowd of gathered Serbs and felt the power he had over them, he decided to become a new Serbian archon. Koca Popovic said about him:

"Milosevic is just a bank rat and a lot of blood will be shed because of him".

Milosevic rejected every possibility of reorganizing the Yugoslav political system. He wasn't interested in loose federation, in confederation, nor in any compromise form of political structure. He clashed with the federal government of the Prime Minister Ante Markovic and stopped the reforms they had initiated, thus stopping the Serbian road to future.

He refused Lord Carrington's plan offered at the meeting with the Presidency of the SFRY in 1991 in Tito's villa in Igalo, where it was suggested that each republic within Yugoslavia could go its independent way. All the leaders of the republics accepted that proposal and Milosevic was the only to reject that plan on confederation. He persuaded his representative, Momir Bulatovic, to withdraw his signature at the Hague Conference, because he said that Montenegro could not get into such Yugoslavia either.

Milosevic wanted Yugoslavia all for himself, even if it was incomplete. He craved to become the president of such country, which was a legal and political successor of the SFRY, so that he could obtain its inheritance – the state property and billions of dollars and Yugoslav gold in foreign banks. The League of Communists of Yugoslavia alone had stored as much as forty-five billion dollars of its party membership fees in foreign banks ever since 1932. Together with other national treasure, there were around seventy-five billion dollars in foreign banks the owner of which was the state of Yugoslavia. In order to snatch that inheritance, Slobodan Milosevic created a new quasi-country, the FRY (Federal Republic of Yugoslavia), and later the State Union of Serbia and Montenegro as the successors of the SFRY.

Fighting for themselves and their family on power, Slobodan Milosevic and his wife Dr Mirjana Markovic became the traitors of communism. They betrayed the ideals of communism, the principles of the labor class self-organization and the rule through equality among all the classes and people. They betrayed justice, truth, and communist honesty. They became autocrats that used communism and Serbdom as excuses for their dictatorship.

The Milosevic family betrayed me, as well, when I came from the USA to Serbia, as an old communist and the citizen of the world, to offer my assistance to it. The Yugoslavia I left in the early seventies was the country of satisfied people, at the world-class standard. The Yugoslavia I came back to in the early nineties was the country of chaos. The return to my homeland enabled me to comprehend the essence of the life in Serbia, but also to discover and comprehend myself – who I was, what I was, and where I was. In such a country, Milosevic, his wife, and other persons on power, robbed me, ruined my business, declared me an American spy, blackmailed me, and threatened to kill me.

THE POLITICS OF DECEIT

In the beginning of the 1990s, the Serbian archon deceived the US State Department that offered him 70 billion dollars for the transition of self-managing public companies into private companies and for the introduction of early capitalism. The USA punished him by imposing international sanctions in 1992 that spawned the criminalization of the country and people, the civil war in former Yugoslav republics, and then the war in 1999 with the NATO, secession in 2008, and the proclamation of the independence of Kosovo and Metohija. Because of the civil war, half a million of the Serbs died, and the NATO bombing destroyed the Serbian country and economy and caused a damage of 100 billion dollars. With the secession of the so-called Kosovo, the Serbian property of at least 300 billion euros was seized. In that way, Slobodan Milosevic destroyed Serbia, Kosmet, and the future of his Serbian people.

He died in the Hague, on 11ᵗʰ March 2006, but he left behind a political legacy burdened with great political, social, and economic issues. He left behind the ruined labor class, devastated country, robbed state, unemployed people, and the political management in a feud with the whole democratic world. In spite of being dead, thanks to the followers of his misdeeds, Milosevic is more alive than ever, and ready to be promoted into a Serbian hero through a monument erection.

Milosevic was an autocrat, a selfish, arrogant, and insolent man, a politically and socially illiterate ruler, and a cruel leader of long-suffering Serbian people. Americans supported him for around ten years as an archon, but Milosevic failed to meet their political expectations – to create new, democratic Yugoslavia and, within it, new, free Serbia.

In my opinion, Slobodan Milosevic is the main culprit for the destruction of Serbia and for losing Kosovo and Metohija, for the humiliation of the Serbs and for bringing them into the situation to be proclaimed a genocidal nation. With his wrongdoing, Milosevic ruined the dignity of the Serbian people and turned them into a minority in their own Kosmet land. And, that is precisely why Slobodan Milosevic has no right to get a monument in the capital city of Serbia.

The problems of inter-national relations between the Serbs and the Albanians, of war conflicts from 1998 and 1999 in Kosovo and Metohija, and the later secession of the Southern province were not attempted to be politically mitigated or solved by the subsequent Serbian leaders, the Prime Minister Zoran Đinđic, the President Vojislav Kostunica, and the President Boris Tadic.

During the ruling of the DOS (Democratic Opposition of Serbia), the relations with the USA were very bad. The President Kostunica, and then Tadic, as well, did not allow the Americans to realize their program of opening the International War Crimes Tribunal in Belgrade, so that our people would be tried in Serbia and that Serbia could be presented as a peacemaker. Instead of peace, Kostunica and Tadic chose war with the USA and the Hague tribunal. After Milosevic, they continued leading bad international politics, because of which Serbia had bad relations with the international community and a bad reputation in the world. Therefore, Aleksandar Vucic, becoming the Prime Minister and, later, the President, was obliged to correct those great mistakes of the government of Milosevic and the DOS.

As the President of Serbia, Vucic appeared in Kosmet in September 2018 precisely with the aim to return the lost dignity and the faith in the future to the Serbian people in the wrested Southern province. By doing so, Vucic returned the faith in better future to all residents of Serbia.

It is quite significant that Vucic received the support of the US President Donald Trump and the US administration, who expressed their devotion to his negotiation efforts, the dialogue with Pristina, and advocating for peace. That also means that after sixteen years, when Milosevic created a dispute with the official Washington and it promoted the socalled independent Kosovo, the USA changed its political and diplomatic attitude towards Serbia. In that manner, a signal was sent to the official Belgrade that they can expect Trump's administration to more considerably change its attitude towards the so-called independent Kosovo.

As a citizen of both the USA and Serbia, on 11th September 2018, via Happy television, I sent a public call to the US Embassy and its personnel to influence the official Washington to reconsider its decision on the so-called independent Kosovo. The fact is, after the visit of Aleksandar Vucic to Kosmet, the US Embassy is in the position to report to Washington that in the so-called independent Kosovo, human rights of Serbian people are being severely violated, the churches and heritage of the Serbian orthodox church are being destroyed, and Serbian private and state property is being wrested in the context of ethnic cleansing.

In Kosovo, with the support of Albanian politicians, warmongering mood toward the Serbian population is gaining strength. The so-called independent Kosovo is becoming a country that is posing a significant danger to the peace and stability in the Balkans and the South-Eastern Europe. Such Kosovo should not be relevant to the national interest of the USA.

If the personnel of the US Embassy in Serbia sent a report from Belgrade to Washington, to the US Secretary of State Mike Pompeo and, in that way, to the President Donald Trump and his administration, on Kosovo as the country where human rights are violated, where there are terroristic threats, and where the leading people are close to the Albanian mafia, a process of revising the US decision on the independence of the Serbian province could be initiated. The revising of the decision of the administrations of George Bush and Bill Clinton, the former presidents of the USA, which would abolish the so-called independent Kosovo as a fake country that is not in the national interest of the USA, would bring a significant political and economic stability to Serbia and the entire region.

As both a Serbian and an American citizen, and as a member of the Republican Party in the USA and a Serbian patriot, with the authority given by the Government of the Republic of Serbia, I am ready to lobby in the USA for the new US administration of the President Donald Trump to reject the decision of the administrations of George Bush and Bill Clinton on recognizing the independence of Kosovo and to return it under the Serbian wing.

This manuscript is my political memoires, more precisely, my perspective from an American viewpoint and from the aspect of Serbian reality of the crucial events from the end of the 20th century in Serbia and the FRY in which the vital role was played by the Serbian archon. My desire is to unveil the truth – who is to blame for the suffering of the Serbian people, what the causes are and what the consequences of the defeat in the war for freedom, national identity, and dignity of the Serbs.

The Author

On Saint Nicolas Day, 2018

МИНИСТАРСТВО ЗА ДИЈАСПОРУ
ВЛАДЕ РЕПУБЛИКЕ СРБИЈЕ
ИМА ПОСЕБНО ЗАДОВОЉСТВО ДА ДОДЕЛИ

ЗАХВАЛНИЦУ

ПРОФ. ДР ЂОРЂЕВИЋ БОРКУ

ЗА АНГАЖОВАЊЕ НА ЗБЛИЖАВАЊУ
МАТИЦЕ И ДИЈАСПОРЕ, ЗАШТИТИ
НАЦИОНАЛНИХ, ВЕРСКИХ, КУЛТУРНИХ
И ЈЕЗИЧКИХ ПРАВА НАШЕГ НАРОДА
У РАСЕЈАЊУ И ПОМОЋИ НАРОДУ СРБИЈЕ ·

У БИОГРАД
13. 10. 2004

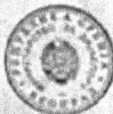

МИНИСТАР

*The Certificate of Appreciation to Dr. Borko Djordjevic from the
Government of Serbia and the Ministry of Diaspora, 2004*

11

THE FATAL WIPING OUT OF THE SERBS

I am neither a politician nor a journalist, but I think that we are now facing the most severe international crisis in Europe since the beginning of the Second World War. NATO has won Montenegro and has started breaking up Bosnia and Herzegovina, as well as Macedonia, the same as it broke up the second Yugoslavia.

During the past thirty years, I have observed the events in the SFRY and Serbia quite carefully. Ever since my return from the USA to Belgrade, in the late 1980s, I have watched Yugoslavia progressively falling apart. I was appalled by the process of dying of a country, but I kept silent. I didn't publicly confront the attitudes that most western politicians and journalists expressed, or their interpretations of the demise of the second Yugoslavia.

I was born in that Yugoslavia. In the 1970s, I went to the USA where I specialized in plastic surgery and achieved a successful medical career. As a former communist that adored the SFRY, I became an American Republican. When the USA and Europe started breaking up Yugoslavia and setting its republics against each other, until the breaking out of a civil war, I was exasperated and disgusted by the images of battles, refugees, and committed atrocities. I always tried to see beyond the broadcast political and media images that just served the political goals.

I constantly felt bitterness and anger caused by the day-to-day prejudices and distortion of facts in the US media. Now, when Yugoslavia doesn't exist anymore, because it was destroyed by NATO bombs, when Serbia is in a serious crisis and struggle for its survival, I finally feel that I have an obligation to speak up. This is my viewpoint on the war the whole world fights against my Serbian people.

In the attempt of NATO to resolve the Kosovo crisis, at the end of 1990s, its politics started becoming more and more unreliable, irrational, and dangerous. This politics still presents a danger now, in the 21st century, not only for the Balkans, but for the whole world. NATO was never an honest mediator in the Balkans. This military alliance is the guardian of the West and its capitalism.

Let us remember that, for instance, peace negotiations in Paris, back in 1995 were directed against the Serbs to that extent that their delegation could not possibly agree with the proposals made there and save at least some dignity and honor. The express aim of NATO was for Kosovo Albanians to accept their proposals and, thus, to isolate the Serbs in order to force them into almost impossible relinquishment or to intentionally provoke them to refuse the proposals. Therefore, ethnic Albanians at least temporarily solved, or pretended to have solved, their internal issues and, for good tactical reasons, used the "peace plan" of NATO as the best way to finally get the separation of the territory of Kosovo and Metohija from Serbia.

At that time, to the terrorists of the Kosovo Liberation Army (KLA), with their explicit territorial pretensions towards the Great Albania, it suited best if Serbia got bombarded. Every centimeter of the land they mined and every bullet their snipers shot was aimed to lead the NATO rockets to the Serbian positions. However, the KLA wasn't a part of the national Albanian government, but a rebellious army of a militaristic and violent separatist movement. So, if the intention of NATO was to drop bombs on the Yugoslav military facilities, one might wonder why it didn't act in the same manner towards the KLA, an organized semi-military power that killed innocent people

Actually, it was highly unlikely that NATO would bombard the KLA because, individually and collectively, western countries did everything in their power firstly to destabilize and, then, to politically and militarily support the disintegration of Yugoslavia. The initiation of the campaign of bombing the FRY was, to put it bluntly, insane. Yugoslavia was a sovereign country. Its government and leaders were defending against an attack according to the international law. If it became an international aggressor and took the side of the rebellious forces, NATO would act just the opposite to the international laws it had committed to abide by. No European sovereign country was attacked from the outside ever since the Soviet invasion of Czechoslovakia in 1968.

NATO doesn't have the mandate of the United Nations to act as the international police force, which it basically is. Many countries that aren't NATO members, fiercely objected to the bombardment, including Russia and China, but also some of its members, such as Italy and Greece. Those countries should have been listened to and not ignored.

The excuse for bombing Serbia was to punish Slobodan Milosevic and his regime, which Jens Stoltenberg, the Secretary General of NATO clearly states today. The operation called *Merciful Angel* simply enabled Americans to show and try out their new war toys.

The final goal of the NATO politics, first during the negotiations, and then through the bombardment campaign, was the support to the Albanian Republic of Kosovo and the Great Albania. That Great Albania, which includes Kosovo and Metohija as well, would inevitably jeopardize Macedonia and, then, Greece, which is exactly what's happening today.

Of all Serbian arguments against the NATO attack and snatching of a part of the territory of the Republic of Serbia, the most striking one is that nothing was resolved in Kosovo and Metohija by threats and bombs. The political state was just aggravated, and additional problems were created in Serbia and in the whole Balkans. The creation of the so-called independent Kosovo dragged the neighboring countries into a political conflict-primarily Macedonia, which already has its long-standing problem of the fast-growing number of citizens that are ethnic Albanians, and which is desperately trying to maintain balance and moderation.

Further waves of the destabilization of Serbia through the so-called independent Kosovo can involve Croatia, Bosnia and Herzegovina, Greece, Bulgaria, Romania, and even Turkey and Italy. What's more, that destabilization doesn't have to be limited to this immediate zone. Russia is a traditional ally of Serbia. Russians perceived the NATO bombing of Serbia as nothing less than an insult, mockery, blow, and provocation. Russia, which has already been made feel vulnerable and weakened, could too easily use the external war to unite its population. That could be quite dangerous for the west that is now attacking Russia through Serbia.

Ever since the disintegration of the Soviet Union at the beginning of 1990s, NATO has gradually been turning into a club of short-sighted and ignorant technocratic bullies disguised as human rights defenders. During the Cold War, there was at least the balance of powers. Now, when Russia is in economic and political confusion, under the impact of the USA and particularly of Great Britain, which has become an agent of the American global imperialism, NATO has become a weapon in the hands of private individuals, leaders of the USA and England, in the first place. NATO did the dirty work in the name of the USA. It was led by Madeleine Albright ("covered in mud, not so bright") and Robin Cook ("the Cock") who claimed that it was "better to do something than nothing at all". Honestly speaking, the images of British or French pilots fighting hand-in-hand against their Serbian colleagues must have been repulsive to everyone remembering the history from the last two world wars when the Serbs were loyal allies to the West and considered to be heroic fighters.

The White House and the Serbian lag in 1918

Through NATO, the West tried to destroy the Serbs and "save the Albanian people". The bombardment caused the increase in the number of refugees, internally displaced persons, separated families, the dead, the crippled, orphans, the destruction of property, buildings, and infrastructure, diseases, and suffering. A severe economic and moral catastrophe was brought down on Serbian people. The war wasn't a moral issue of a fight between the right against the wrong, the good against the bad, as it was claimed by the leaders of NATO countries. The conflict in Kosovo and Metohija is a complex inter-ethnical, inter-tribal civil war with a long history. It flared in the region in the villages of which there is an endemic tradition of revenge, vendetta, and blood feud, which was the only law less than a century ago.

The NATO leaders didn't read, experience, or understand that history and weren't even interested in doing so. In the Balkan conflict –as in any other conflict – fighting occurs between fallible and ignorant human beings, where each side, with its deeply-rooted ideology and system of values, believes that their cause is just. It is obvious to everyone, except to the imperialistic rulers of the NATO countries, that such conflict cannot be "resolved" by simple external imposing of moral values of the western liberal ideology – in this case, literally from above, i.e. by bombs dropped from the sky. It takes a high level of patience, modesty, and understanding, which people like Clinton and Blair were obviously completely incapable of.

Besides, the western military alliance is neither an army of salvation, nor an army of justice. The list of injustices, shameful deeds, and atrocities approved, tolerated, sponsored, or even directly committed by the NATO countries in the past thirty years is a rather long one. Here are a few examples. The West did nothing in order to protect the population of Northern Cyprus from the Turkish invasion and Turkey is a NATO member. No international army ever went to resolve the constant disturbances in Northern Ireland, and Americans secretly sponsored the IRA like they assisted the KLA. NATO didn't lift a finger when Israel persecuted Palestinians, expanded to the left side of the Jordan and occupied Gaza and Southern Lebanon. It did nothing to help the Kurds in Turkey or the Serbs in mass persecutions from Krajina in Croatia. That is why the motives of the NATO countries for intervening in Kosovo should be considered deeply suspicious.

Just the announcement of the bombardment of Serbia, in the mid-nineties, drove out the aid-providing agencies from the FRY and Kosovo and Metohija, paving the way to the two warring sides to really strike one another. The bare bomb threat made the situation in the Southern Province irreparable. The Serbs and the Albanians made war and NATO already took the suitable stand to blame the Serbs. The western propaganda machinery was already lubricated to pump out as many lies as possible in an exceptionally efficient and credible manner. I carefully observed western media during the Yugoslav conflict. From the moment it seemed that Yugoslavia could disintegrate, our politicians, journalists, and TV commentators had a strong tendency to present the Serbs as villains and all the others were looked at through rose-colored glasses. Whenever the accusations, which were constantly directed against Serbs, could be directed against Croatians, Bosnian Muslims, and now ethnic Albanians in Kosovo, they were in a certain manner reduced to minimum or overseen. All the inhumanities, crimes, and atrocities of the Albanians, Croatians, and Bosnians were quite well "laundered" and covered up, and they were acquitted of the charges. But, on the other hand, the Serbs were demonized.

Just among the leading British politicians, the Serbs were demonized by Margaret Thatcher, David Owen, Paddy Ashdown, Tony Blair, Robin Cook, and George Robertson. The only leading British politicians that I heard speaking modestly, intelligently, and reasonably about Yugoslavia were Lord Carrington, Tony Benn, and George Galloway.

The history says that, during the time of Josip Broz Tito, the imbalance of the population in Kosovo and Metohija arose from its gradual albanization and encouraging Serbs to leave the province. From 1940 that was a slow, consistent, and gradual ethnic cleansing of the Serbs, which was program-based and organized by Tito's government and aided and supported by well-documented examples of anti-Serbian behavior of the local Albanians. Until the breakup of Yugoslavia, Serbian population suffered rapes, murders, atrocities, massacres, and ethnic cleansing by Albanian nationalists. It is an obvious lie spread by NATO that the Serbs were the only ones to blame for the disintegration of the SFRY and Bosnia and Herzegovina. The blame is also on Muslims, Croats, Slovenians, and Albanians, at least the individuals that caused the war and committed atrocities over the Serbian population. The NATO countries assisted them in that.

Croatia, with the assistance of the USA, quite successfully ethnically cleansed its territory by expatriating Serbs from Krajina, who were, in addition to that, stoned along their way in their lines on the road to Serbia. Serbs had been accused of wanting the Great Serbia and the West then implicitly supported the Great Albania.

A lot of weaponry came through Europe and it was financed by western sources for the needs of Croatian, Bosnian, and Albanian armies. Germany was one of the most prominent powers that adopted the approach of active destabilization of Yugoslavia. Through their Minister of Foreign Affairs, Genscher, when the Berlin Wall was pulled down, the political leaders of the newly-formed Germany were the first to recognize the independence of Slovenia, Croatia, and Bosnia and Herzegovina, which suited their "divide and conquer" economic politics in the Central and Eastern Europe. Hans-Dietrich Genscher considered the destruction of the SFR of Yugoslavia his supreme professional achievement.

The politics of the New World Order, NATO, the USA, and the EU reduced to the political credo: "Hit Serbs", at the end of the 20th century, turned into a pure rage, the only aim the West was thinking about, and into a campaign of the extremely selective persecution of the Serbs. If I sit down with my head cool and wonder why all that happened, it is quite hard to think of a logical or clear answer.

What was the real motivation for that? What psychology of the world rulers is behind all that? Can the persecution of the Serbs be compared to anti-Semitism? Bill Clinton already had the audacity to compare himself with Winston Churchill and Slobodan Milosevic with Adolf Hitler. Was Slobodan Milosevic really the "Butcher of the Balkans" that it was necessary to get rid of him by retaliating against Serbs? If that was the case, Milosevic definitely wasn't a dictator any worse than the leaders of Croatia, Slovenia, Bosnia and Herzegovina, and Albania, or maybe of Turkey and Saudi Arabia that persecuted minorities in their countries.

Economic sanctions were not imposed on any of these countries, none of which possesses a particularly nice history in respect to human rights, nor a democratic tradition. In Serbia, there was a students' protest as a proof of a strong libertarian and anti-authoritative tradition, but that movement was never encouraged or incited by anyone in the West.

Serbian students knew that Slobodan Milosevic traded Serbian population as if they had been goods, that he spent summer holidays in Greece with Franjo Tuđman, the Croatian President, both officially and informally, , and that they discussed the division of Yugoslavia and expatriation of the Serbs from Dinara and Slavonija. The activists in the students' protest in 1996 knew that Milosevic's delegation, led by Professor Smilja Avramov, negotiated with Tuđman's delegation on the division of territories in Bosnia and Herzegovina, while Vukovar was on ire. That was actually a plan on the ethnic cleansing of Bosnia and Herzegovina.

Students that protested against Slobodan Milosevic and his family on power knew that his wife, comrade Mira Markovic, as a communist leader, was taking out the Yugoslav wealth to Japan and Russia. They saw that their children, daughter Marija and son Marko, learned the lesson of seizing national treasure from the Serbian people to obtain personal gain.

Personally, it seems to me, looking from the American viewpoint, as a resident of California, and from the Serbian viewpoint, as a resident of Belgrade, that the war of the West against the Serbs and NATO bombing has a close connection with the control of the FRY territory, i.e. Serbia and Montenegro, and then the area of the entire former SFRY. There lies the simplest key for breaking up Serbs as the greatest and most influential people in the Balkans.

NATO wants to control the whole Balkans, to turn the whole region into a series of puppet states, thus controlling the Mediterranean from the Black Sea to the Gibraltar. The Serbs were on the way to the new world order reflected in the NATO army. That's why the NATO leaders ordered: Wipe the Serbs out of the Balkans map!

Bill Clinton and Toni Blair, as well as other rulers from NATO, were smiling sinisterly as they were accomplishing this goal. They were accomplishing it from two levels: personally, through the presidents that were very obedient, Alija Izetbegovic, Franjo Tuđman, and Slobodan Milosevic, and officially, through their negotiators and peace-makers, such as the Ambassador Richard Holbrooke, and through the commanders of the NATO forces. Both levels of the realization of the plan "Wipe Serbs out of the Balkans map!" were conducted in the combination of emotional pleasure and professional indifference with which politicians and generals analyzed military capacities for the destruction of the Serbian people and the results of that political campaign.

This pattern is repeated today in the international community that "cares" for Kosmet, and for Macedonia as well. The USA, the EU, and NATO are sincerely indifferent towards the fate of the Albanians, Macedonians, Bosnians, and Serbs in the problematic countries of the Balkans – Kosmet, Macedonia, Bosnia and Herzegovina, and Serbia.

This political and military pattern, tested on Serbs, is started being applied on Russia and the Russian people. Through the western propaganda, they are now actively being inserted into the story on the Serbs and the Albanians, on the Serbs and the Bosnians, and on Macedonia, which is allegedly a Russian influence zone. In order to avoid new sufferings inflicted by NATO, we need to use our heads and work independently.

The Serbs and the Albanians must communicate at any cost. There is no other way. If the Americans and the English dropped bombs again, the worst bully and barbarian of all will actually be NATO, because, in the world alliance, NATO only cares about the Serbs to disappear forever. With that secret aim, the EU is leading peace negotiations between Belgrade and Pristina today. That is absolutely clear to me. And to you?

There is no doubt that, in the future, the USA, Great Britain, and other developed countries of NATO will discover and use other similar molds, as necessary, especially when it comes to finding a desirable arena that is not too close to home, in order to try out more sophisticated ("smart") weapons. Unfortunately, the truth is more deranged and worse than the presented image. For their own false purposes, NATO intentionally stirs the complex, but localized conflict so that it becomes an enormous and more venomous international fabrication, whose capacity of causing effects of cyclic impacts cannot be easily foreseen by its leaders. That's not just irresponsible. That's evil. If I was a Serb – and I don't mean a supporter of Milosevic – I would be quite furious because of the injustice towards my personal and cultural heritage, so I would feel I have no other choice but to defend my country from the NATO aggression. If I was a Kosovo Albanian, I would probably lead a campaign for the termination of Serbian dominance and I would support or join the KLA. We have been told that the Serbs are the greatest bullies in the region, but that is far from the truth. The KLA sees the justice turning towards them, in a long term, and they are ready to quibble and provoke in every way in order to promote their cause, believing their cause to be just. The Serbs are surrounded and defensive, but that won't stop them from fighting, no matter who's leading them, because they are far from being cowards and Kosovo is their homeland and they, too, believe their cause is just.

A LAWSUIT AGAINST BILL CLINTON

When the Prime Minister Ana Brnabic met the President of the USA Donald Trump at the session of the UN General Assembly in New York in 2018, she thanked him for the change of the relation the current administration in Washington had towards Serbia and for the understanding they had shown in respect to the attitudes of our country towards Kosovo and Metohija. The first man of the USA responded to that in the following manner:

"Serbs are good people."

According to the impressions of political reporters from the session of the UN General Assembly, the USA is ready to re-examine the Kosovo issue and, if Belgrade and Pristina reach an agreement, they will accept it.

Until this summer, that was unimaginable, because Washington considered the Kosovo issue a closed book. However, the visit of our officials to the USA in July and the ceremony of marking a century since Serbian lag was first raised on the White House, as well as the diplomatic efforts of the President Aleksandar Vucic, have cast a different light on the relations of the two countries and they have moved on a different path.

The President Donald Trump has changed the attitude of Washington towards Serbia to a certain extent because he distanced himself from the war politics of the USA in the 1990s that was led by the US presidents George Bush and Bill Clinton. Rejecting their political heritage, which tarnished the reputation of the USA in the world, President Trump opened the door for a dialogue with Serbia and gave us the possibility to make an agreement with the Albanians in Kosovo and Metohija, indicating that the USA would respect such an agreement. We should use this chance given by the official Washington.

However, we should have a precise plan how to return Kosmet and we should discuss that with the Americans. They are ready to make a concession to Serbia. To my mind, one plan would be to initiate the process of the revision of the decision of Clinton's administration on the Albanian secession of Kosovo and Metohija with the assistance of the US Embassy in Belgrade, through Mike

Pompeo, the US Secretary of State, whom I'm personally well-acquainted with. This process isn't impossible, because it exists in the legal system of the USA and it can be implemented.

The US President Donald Trump and the Serbian Prime Minister Ana Brnabic

My other plan is to file a lawsuit against the former government of the USA and former presidents George Bush and Bill Clinton for their seizing Serbian private and state property in Kosovo and Metohija and for its returning to Serbs. Such lawsuits have already been filed against the State Department and the US residents and they had positive outcomes - the return of the property to the states of Panama and Iran, which had been taken with the concordance and in the jurisdiction of the USA.

Borko Djordjevic, MD, a Republican and a surgeon

One Serbian lawsuit was positively resolved in the USA, as well. That is a well-known case of the Serbs from Krajina, who sued the retired US generals from the MPRI organization in the USA for participating in the operation Storm in the summer of 1995. The first lawsuit was filed by the citizens Lizabet Lalic and Bogdan Kljaic from Krajina. In a collective lawsuit in the Federal Court in 2010, a group of Serbs from Krajina sued the generals for non-pecuniary damages, for pain and suffering caused by losing the homeland. They sought 10.4 billion dollars, plus the interest since 1995 on the basis of the complicity in genocide reflected in around 2,000 dead and missing and 200,000 persecuted persons, destructing, pillaging, seizing property and preventing their return.

In the lawsuit, Serbs refer to the fact that the MPRI advised, trained and, violating the embargo, secretly equipped the Croatian army with sophisticated weapons for the operation *Storm*. As evidence, they submitted to the court the contracts between the MPRI and Croatia on the training of Croatian officers and soldiers.

The request for damages for being forced to leave their homes was based on the case of the Japanese in the USA who, after the bombardment of Pearl Harbor, were placed in camps, and were later awarded 25,000 each by the court for pain and suffering.

The Serbs were represented by three American legal companies with around eighty lawyers, who will charge their representation services upon the finalization of the dispute in the amount of one third of the overall sum received in the court's final decision or settlement, which is common in such cases in the USA.

From the legal perspective, the Serbian lawsuit against the former presidents George Bush and Bill Clinton, whose political decisions caused the secession of the Albanians, the separation of the Serbian southern province from Serbia, the creation of the so-called independent Kosovo, and the seizing of the property of Serbian citizens, could be filed at several US courts and, finally, at the Supreme Court of the USA. In the first instance, the lawsuit would be filed by the American citizens of Serbian origin, i.e. Serbs from Kosmet, whose property was seized, unlawfully appropriated, used, or sold by Albanians after the creation of the so-called independent Kosovo. Then, lawsuits should be filed by Serbian organizations, such as, e.g. the Serbian Orthodox Church – its eparchies in the USA and Serbia – whose monasteries and churches, estates, and immovable property were stolen.

Formally and legally, according to the US laws, Serbian lawsuit could not refer to the military attack of the USA on Serbia, the responsibility of Clinton and Bush for the bombardment and ethnic cleansing in 1999 in Serbia, because there is no law in the USA according to which anyone could be taken liable for that. In that way, Americans prevented their statesmen and generals from being taken to the International Court for War Crimes. That is why the USA and its presidents weren't taken to court for the bombardment of Vietnam, Korea, and the FRY.

Americans made Kosmet their 51st state, but on the European soil. In that manner, they are undermining the EU, weakening Germany, and causing the instability of Europe. Money is everything in the American world domination politics. President Bill Clinton charged the Albanians well for the creation of the so-called independent Kosovo. The members of Clinton's administration, Madeleine Albright, General Wesley Clark, and others opened their companies in Kosmet. Their aim was to extract national treasure from Kosovo and Metohija and to get rich.

US President Gerald Ford and Dr. Borko Djordjevic

THE STOLEN OWNERSHIP RIGHT

The lawsuit against Bill Clinton would deal only and exclusively with the issue of the violation of human rights, i.e. the ownership right of the Serbs, the usurpation of private property of the Serbs, unlawful seizing of real estate, property, companies, and livelihood of the Serbs and other residents of the so-called Kosovo due to the causes arising from the state politics of former presidents of the USA and the consequence that the stolen property is worth around 300 billion euros.

The question of ownership of land and other immovable property is quite relevant to the Americans and Donald Trump will understand such Serbian request. The USA want to get rid of Thaçi and Haradinaj and bring to power younger, more moderate people, who don't have the résumé of war terrorists and mobsters. Serbia should use that opportunity.

However, the situation with the Serbian property isn't great. Slobodan Milosevic is to blame for that. His biggest mistake was that he didn't conduct the restitution of the property in Kosovo and Metohija. If he had returned the taken and usurped property to monasteries, the land Albanians had taken would have been returned to the Serbs and many problems wouldn't even exist today and the negotiating position of Serbia over the Kosovo issue would be radically better.

At the beginning of the 21st century, the Serbian Unity Congress from the USA first started dealing with the institutional and legal aspects of the taken property and possessions of the Serbian people in Kosmet. Then, Mrs. Mirjana Samardzija, Mr. Miroslav Djordjevic and Priest Irinej Dobrijevic pointed to the of icial Washington and particularly to congressmen and senators visiting Kosmet, that Albanian nationalists, whether they were politicians or neighbors, were seizing private property of the Serbs. And, they were also stealing the property and houses of the Serbs persecuted from Kosmet to Central Serbia or abroad and even of some US citizens. This Serbian organization submitted to the US Congress the complete documentation with the names of thousands of Serbs who had lost their property, ields, meadows, houses, and companies in Kosmet.

From 1,088,699 hectares of land the Serbs had a warranty deed upon, according to the cadastre records, more than 80% was usurped by the Albanians. The value of that land is ifty billion dollars. The Brussels Agreement envisages that, when the inal agreement is reached, *the seized land* is to be returned to the people persecuted from Kosovo and Metohija.

With the creation of the so-called Kosovo in 2008 the banishment of the Serbs from the province was accelerated and the seizing of Serbian state property was activated. Unfortunately, apart from the Albanian forces, international organizations such as the UN, KFOR, EULEX, UNMIK, and NATO, as well as the USA participated in that. The Americans, for instance, made their military base Camp Bondsteel on the private property of the Serbs from Urosevac.

If it is a well-known fact that Serbs are the owners of 90% of the land and that the country of Serbia is the owner of the majority of companies, then, it is clear that most of the property in Kosmet is Serbian. The Americans perfectly understand that fact and they should become interested in bringing it back to reality, so that the Serbs could be the owners of their own property again.

THE ROBBERY OF THE INTERNATIONAL COMMUNITY

From 1961 to 1990, Serbia invested 17.6 billion dollars into Kosovo and Metohija, which is around 600 million dollars per year.

Starting in 1966, Yugoslavia allocated 1.5 to 2% of its GDP for the development of insuf iciently developed areas and the largest portion of those funds was directed to Kosmet.

In the years immediately before the disintegration of the SFRY, as much as 48% of the funds allocated for the underdeveloped went to Kosovo and Metohija and most of it was invested in energetics and non-ferrous metallurgy. Looking at the documents, the situation is clear –the Development Fund of the Republic of Serbia has a share in the Kosmet property of 55% to 65%, and 20% is the social capital that belonged to the employees. Therefore, there should be no problems in establishing, for instance, who is the majority owner of 1,358 facilities in Kosovo that belong to the companies from Serbia. However, unfortunately, that isn't the case.

In the framework for negotiations with the EU, it states that the facilities and property of the state companies that didn't enter the process of privatization until 2008 belong to Kosovo and that all other companies belong to Serbia. However, the problem is that there are few such companies and little such land. Most Serbian companies are sold in the criminal process of privatization, whose foundation is laid in the Privatization Regulation declared in 2005 by Søren Jessen-Petersen, the head of the UNMIK at the time. Believe it or not, that document stipulates that it is not necessary to determine the origin of ownership, but that it can be done after the sale, through a court. The UNMIK entrusted the privatization of the state property found in Kosmet to the Kosovo Property Agency (KPA). Thus, the KPA became the owner of 720 state and all the 6 public companies: Pristina Airport, the Regional Heating Company in Đakovica and in Pristina, Kosovo Energetic Corporation, Kosovo Post Of ices and Telecommunication, Railway, Water Supply, Sewage, and Irrigation Company.

This unprecedented robbery is performed under the auspices of the United Nations, even though the Resolution 1244 of the UN Security Council doesn't envisage any participation of the UN in the changing of ownership rights in Kosovo and Metohija. Contrary to the de inition stating that the ownership rights of the state and of legal and natural persons cannot be altered without their explicit consent, the UNMIK arbitrarily and contrary to the Resolution 1244 of the UN Security Council usurped the ownership rights and possession over the immovable property and companies. Thus, a large part of the property of Serbian companies was "privatized" under the cover of the alleged "99-year-long lease". Such privatization isn't legal and shouldn't have any legal repercussions to the country of Serbia, especially because Serbia, as the majority owner, was all along paying the foreign debt of Kosovo, which amounted to 1.7 billion euros. However, unfortunately, according to the system "might makes right", our country can only seek its ownership rights though the Supreme Court of Kosovo. Until now, around 200 companies from Serbia have addressed that court, but they have no rights in this wild privatization, as claimed by the UNMIK and Kosovo authorities. Nevertheless, the Serbian Chamber of Commerce considers that the right to the property worth more than 300 billion euros should not be renounced and that the country must demand from the relevant international institutions to annul the privatization process in Kosovo.

Gazivode Lake

In my opinion, Kosmet was turned into a country, a foreign colony to be precise, so that the western forces could extract mineral resources out of it. There are large reserves of it estimated at several hundreds of billions of euros: lignite, lead, zinc, nickel, cobalt, magnesite, bauxite, natural gas, and rare metal ores. The CIA estimated that the natural wealth is worth 500 billion dollars.

The largest rock- illed dam in Europe, built during Tito's rule, which cost over 900 million dollars, is the main loot of the Albanian authorities today. Belgrade company *Hydrotechnics – hydroenergentics* built it from 1973 to 1977 in the area of Gazivode Village as one of the largest dams in Europe with clay foundation, according to the design of *Energoproject*, a company from Belgrade. The cornerstone for the construction of the dam and the creation of the arti icial lake Gazivode was placed on Saint Peter's Day in 1972. Gazivode is the property of the Republic of Serbia, i.e. EPS (Electric Power Industry of Serbia).

Gazivode Lake has around 380,000 cubic meters of water. The whole north of Kosovo and Metohija, Kosovska Mitrovica, Zvecan, Zubin Potok, Vucitrn, and the municipality of Srbica are supplied with water from this lake. And, the thermal power plant in Obilic could not work without the water from Gazivode that cools the plants that produce electric energy. Although Pristina uses fraud in relation to ownership and requests to include the lake into the energy system of Kosmet and to let the Albanians manage Gazivode, and to resolve the ownership issue later, Serbia is determined not to let the Albanians have the majority management.

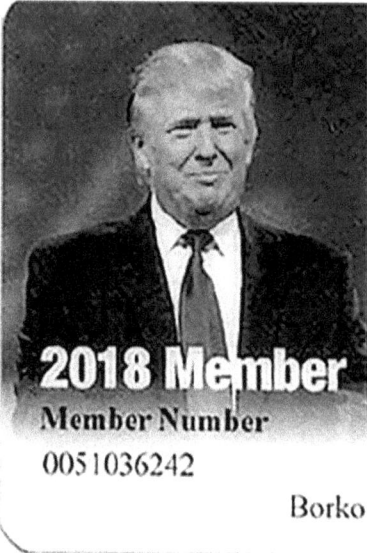

01-046696

The Conservative Caucus

I Stand With President Trump Against The Coup!

Signature

Member Number
0051036242

Member Since
12/17

2018 Member

Borko Djordjevic

Borko Djordjevic - a member of the Trump's Republican Party, 2018

SEIZING THE DAM AND LAKE

The arti icial lake and hydroelectric power plant are the apple of discord because the one who controls them, controls the energetic resources for the north of Kosovo, but also the water resources for the territory of the entire Kosovo and Metohija. Despite the fact that 74% of the lake is on the territory of the municipality Zubin Potok and 25.9%on the territory of Novi Pazar and Tutin, Pristina claims that it is their property.

According to the Kosmet media, Pristina has already sold the entire electrical distribution and network, including Gazivode, to a Turkish company that demands to get what they have paid for, but cannot get into the possession of the lake and hydroelectric power plant.

The President of Serbia, Aleksandar Vucic, visited Gazivode in September 2018 in order to send a clear message to Pristina and the international community that nobody can seize private and state property of the Republic of Serbia. Gazivode Lake is mostly located on the territory of Serbia and in a minor part on the territory of Kosovo and its accumulation is quite signi icant for the economic life, agriculture, thermal power plant and for the entire Serbia and its energetic future.

Aleksandar Vucic is ready to deal with all the issues that the Serbs and other citizens in Kosmet might have. In order to get the people and the country out of problems, Vucic must provide the continuity of long rule in order to be able to conduct his plan of the development of Serbia in the long run. At the same time, the President needs to stop all the discords that exist among the Serbs, among political parties and their leaders, between the Serbs in the homeland and the ones in emigration. He needs to bring the people from diaspora back to Serbia. All the Serbs in the world must unite and build new Serbia together. Hungarians did so, they brought their diaspora back home and created modern Hungary.

When János Kádár, the President of Hungary, signed a pact with the USSR in 1954, around 3.5 million Hungarians emigrated. When Orbán came to power, Hungarian emigrants returned home to help in the development of Hungary. That is how the country of Serbia should behave and it should return the emigrants home with its politics of cooperation with diaspora. Serbia should be whole and united. All the Serbs from emigration should return to it and, together with the Serbs in the homeland, get involved in the program of the development of Serbia.

In case of the lawsuit against George Bush and Bill Clinton for the return of the Serbian property in Kosmet, the Serbs from the USA and the whole diaspora should ile it, but also the Serbs from Serbia, as well as all other citizens of our country that lost their property. When the Supreme Court of the USA receives ive thousand lawsuits against Bush and Clinton, it certainly won't dismiss them, and it will open a process on their liability for the violation of human and ownership rights of Kosovo and Metohija residents.

THE PRESIDENT AND THE COMMUNIST TRANSITION

I am a metropolitan child that inished the Fifth Belgrade Grammar School and the Faculty of Medicine. I was the party secretary to my professors and fellow students. Since I was a Communist, it took me three attempts to inally get the US visa to go to my grandfather Sava in New Jersey. I went to the USA in the early 1970s and specialized in plastic surgery. I also did some business, because in the USA everything is about the money – good life, work, career, and reputation.

Being a surgeon, I had a privilege to beautify the faces of the irst ladies of the USA. My patients were Betty Ford, the wife of President Gerald Ford, then Rosalynn Carter, the wife of President Jimmy Carter, Nancy Reagan, the wife of President Ronald Reagan, as well as Ivana Trump, the irst wife of President Donald Trump.

When I got politically active as a Republican, I became a functionary in the cabinet of Ronald Reagan, the Governor of California and then the President of the USA. I am a member of the Carter Center through which I took the former President Jimmy Carter to Pale in 1994 and made the irst peace in Bosnia and Herzegovina that lasted four and a half months.

In the '90s, I was the of icial envoy of the Republic of Srpska in the USA. Ronald Reagan awarded me the Medal for Merit for my contribution to the Republican Party and George Bush awarded me with the Medal for Special Merits in the USA and an engraved gold watch. President Barack Obama is now my neighbor in Palm Springs.

Jovan Zebic, Buca Prohaska, Dr Borko Djordjevic, and Schmidt Chiari, the President of the Creditanstalt

I returned to Belgrade for the irst time at the end of 1980s and met my school mates and old friends. In Belgrade, my friend Mihajlo Misko Jeremic, the director of *Jugopetrol* and the father of Vuk Jeremic, revealed to me that Yugoslavia was facing great challenges. It was supposed to initiate the reform of the state system and to transform communism into capitalism as innocuously as possible. The transition of the SFRY was initiated and advocated by the Yugoslav Prime Minister Ante Markovic.

Jeremic asked for my assistance, to engage my American colleagues from the Republican Party, my friends in the US Congress and Senate, and my acquaintances in the world of business. Together, we considered the offer of the companies *Texaco* and *Shell* to privatize the state company *Jugopetrol*. The offers arrived for the privatization of *RTS, Energopetrol, EI Nis*, and many other large Yugoslav and Serbian state companies.

On one occasion, I got introduced to the Serbian President Slobodan Milosevic and repeated the story on the privatization of Yugoslav companies to him. I brought Goldstein Jett, the representative of *Motorola*, to support Slobodan Milosevic and his reform of the Serbian economy. We appeared at CNN together.

I spent time with Janez Drnovsek from Slovenia at the business summit in Davos. He publicly spoke that Communists in the SFRY need to turn into Democrats. In April 1990, when Janez Drnovsek was the president of Yugoslavia, I was arranging with him to enable Motorola company to enter the SFRY and conduct the privatization of *EI Nis, RTS,* and *PTT.*

My friend, Buca Prohaska, hired me as his privatization advisor and, in that capacity, I communicated with the Serbian Prime Minister Dragutin Zelenovic, the Belgrade Mayor Milorad Unkovic, and visited Miki Savicevic, the director of *Geneks.* I organized the Serbian delegation's trip to Davos to the summit of world leaders and businessmen. I connected Buca Prohaska with the Americans.

With the privatization, the restoration of the communist economy would start and its transformation into capitalistic property relations and coming out to the free world market. The recipe was quickly feasible and painless in respect to the social peace and state system.

The US Ambassador at the time was John Scanlan, who excellently spoke the Serbian language and went to Saint Day's celebrations because he loved the Serbs and supported Slobodan Milosevic. He believed that Sloba, as a modern politician, understood the need for the great transition in Serbia and he sent positive reports on Milosevic to the White House and State Department. "Milosevic is a modern man, a banker. He wants changes. He is a democrat because he organized the irst multi-party elections..." wrote Ambassador Scanlan.

Ambassador Scanlan opened the door to the entry of the US capital into the drug factory *Galenika* and enabled its privatization. When the new US Ambassador Warren Zimmermann came to Belgrade in 1989, he continued making efforts into conducting the accelerated American privatization of Yugoslavia and Serbia. Unfortunately, the reality showed that this American, who had previously had of ice in Croatia, didn't get into the essence of the Serbian nature. We, the Serbs, are inherently forest people, *haiduks* who prefer plundering to working and earning. We, the Serbs, behave today the same as *haiduks* did during the time of the Prince Milos.

We work from May to November and, then, we enjoy and rampage, stealing state property, budget, and funds in order to survive the winter. Such behavior that saved us from Turks is in our genes and our greatest law. We, the Serbs, the same as *haiduks*, cannot put up with leaders. Whenever there's a new leader, we remove him. We can only put up with one archon because we expect him to work instead of us and take us to the future.

At that point, in 1990 and 1991, there was no knowledge, understanding, or readiness to start the transition in the American way. The Serbs chose, as usually, the blood path of changes. And what happened?

On 9th March 1991, Serbian opposition, led by Vuk Draskovic, performed a coup at Serbia and Milosevic's state system. The Mister of Police Radmilo Bogdanovic responded to the opposition and the violent demonstrators with water cannons and the new Yugoslav President Bora Jovic used tanks. It was clear to the Americans and the entire west that, by doing so, Slobodan Milosevic opted against the changes and for the preservation of communism.

In order to preserve Yugoslavia, as a political creation, and its property, Milosevic busted into the state budget of the SFRY and took seven billion dollars and, then, put all the money in Serbia under his control.

Jimmy Carter in a conversation with Dr. Borko Djordjevic

A NEST IN *GENEX* APARTMENTS

In the early '90s, I worked as a plastic surgeon in a rented surgery of the Department of Gynecology and Obstetrics in the Clinical Centre "Dragisa Misovic" in Dedinje. At the time, I cooperated with Dr Stanoje Glisic. I operated the members of Serbian elite such was, for instance, Rođa, a singer. I beautified a singer Ana Bekuta, as well. I had sold everything I had in the USA wishing to expand my business in Yugoslavia. Unfortunately, there was no real medical work for me. I was sitting in *Genex Apartments,* for which I was paying a rent of 350 Deutsche marks, and watching how the Serbian economy of a banker Slobodan Milosevic was functioning.

Genex Apartments in New Belgrade were the center of all the smuggling and deceiving of the Serbian people. There were Milosevic's owners and traders of the black market, the organizers of smuggling of various goods from Greece, Macedonia, Bulgaria, Turkey, and Hungary, as well as fake bankers known as Da ina and Jezda. They lived like little gods. Dafina Milanovic and her pyramidal bank *Dafiment* led by Mihalj Kertes, the first person of the Customs Administration, and Jezdimir Vasiljevic, the infamous Gazda Jezda ("Jezda the Boss"), and his bank *Jugoskandik* led by Jovica Stanisic, the head of the Serbian Secret Police. When Dafina Milanovic moved in, there formed endless lines of people waiting for money.

Zeljko Raznatovic Arkan used to come to Dafina. Everyone from her surroundings and from the state leadership was saying that he was an "okay guy". I didn't know what that meant, but it was clear to me that the state leadership was robbing their own people through Dafina and Jezda. The pyramidal banks with fake high interests were a mass deceit of people, which was conducted by Slobodan Milosevic with his clique.

In *Genex Apartments*, opposite my of ice, there was the office of *Delta* company which had only two employees. The owner was Miroslav Miskovic. There, in the luxurious *Genex Apartments*, in the wing of power, that first Serbian tycoon was created. In Genex, I met Zoran Kojic, the director of the *Intercontinental*

Hotel. There were also some, to me, odd people: a Marcetic, who wanted to buy a casino in the *Intercontinental* Hotel, then a Mr. Jablan, who was murdered, there was also Mr. Radonjic, who worked with the General Badza.

Milosevic wanted to rule as a dictator. He fought for Serbia as a lioness fights for her cub. At that time he was supported by the Americans because they believed he could change his mind and, as a banker with western manners, move towards transition. I personally believed that Slobodan Milosevic would open to the West and conduct the transition. That is why I assisted Milosevic and my friends, as an éminence grise from the USA, in replacing communism with democracy.

Most of those Milosevic's people from the glass nest of the SPS in *Genex Apartments* observed me just as an American sheep for fleecing.

"Hey doctor, you're a millionaire. Why don't you give a dollar or two for Serbia! Help us survive this unfair embargo imposed by Americans and Europeans" – people from *Genex Apartments* would say to me.

Some of them did that honestly and with good intentions, and the others in a perfidious manner, just to provoke and humiliate me. To them, the power they were obtaining through the country and money gave the right to present themselves as the masters of the FRY and Serbia.

"I will help, by all means. Serbia is my homeland, as well, not just yours," I would answer.

Apart from having numerous professional obligations, as a Serbian patriot, I wished to use the moment of good cooperation between Serbia and the USA and persuade my former communist comrades to move into transition in the American way. I reminded them that Zivorad Kovacevic, the Yugoslav Ambassador in Washington, in 1988, conveyed to the official Belgrade the US offer to the SFRY to buy the military equipment and weapons for the military aviation of the YNA through the multinational company *KPMG*. The offer reached General Jovan Matovic and it was worth 3 billion dollars.

In 1989, the Yugoslavian PTT community was offered a job worth 200 million dollars to privatize and modernize this company. I mediated in this business, which failed due to political reasons.

SLOBA DECEIVED THE AMERICANS

From the moment I returned to Serbia to the end of the 1990s, I met Slobodan Milosevic, his wife Mira Markovic, their son Marko, and their daughter-in-law Milica on several occasions. The first time I visited Milosevic officially was with Schmidt Chiari, the President of the Creditanstalt, at the beginning of 1990, when this bank intended to open a Belgrade branch. It was a chance for a quick development of Serbia.

Slobodan Milosevic always votes 'AGAINST'

During the elections in 1990, I brought two senators, the Deputy Mayor of New York, and around twenty businessmen to Serbia. The night before the elections, President Slobodan Milosevic received them. That convinced me that Sloba wished an honest cooperation with the Americans.

During 1991, I corresponded with Director Selimir Savic from *Genex* in relation to the cooperation with *Federal Express Europlex*, a company from Brussels, and their opening of a branch of ice in Belgrade. The material and meeting were being prepared for the end of January 1991 in Brussels regarding the entrance of *Federal Express* in Yugoslavia. I also represented *Nynex* company in Serbia.

I created the possibility for the US millionaire Rose Mihata, a woman very close to the English royal court and very influential in business and political circles, to get involved in the Serbian business. Ms. Mihata was a well-known humanitarian and the representative of a foundation helping disabled children around the world.

I was also an associate of the Washington trust *KPMG* and its representative Peat Marwick in Serbia.

For the Americans, Serbia in the early nineties was the most important business partner in the Balkans. To be specific, according to the analysis of *KPMG*, the free economic market in Yugoslavia, which was dominated by Serbia, was rather poorly developed. Two ownership types were prevalent, state and public ownership, while the private property was present to a lesser degree. Since 1988, owing to the Prime Minister Ante Markovic, the laws were passed enabling the development of the economic market and the privatization process in the SFRY. That is why KPMG chose to directly participate, in the name of the US Government, in the reform of the economy and state companies in Serbia first.

The Americans wanted to perform the property transition of Yugoslavia and, at the same time, to make an excellent deal in Serbia. They wanted to pay the full price of healthy Serbian state companies and smaller enterprises and privatize them. The main investor of the privatization in Serbia was supposed to be the multinational company *KPMG*. That is an American trust managed by the Masons and Jews, through which they rule the USA.

Luckily, some of my former communist comrades and members of the ruling Socialist Party of Serbia (SPS) listened to me and accepted the cooperation with the American trust *KPMG* regarding the reform and privatization of the Serbian economy.

I have the letter of *KPMG* corporation in my possession in which, at the end of 1991, it offers to the Government of Serbia the investments of 40 billion dollars in largest Serbian enterprises and 30 billion dollars in the privatization of the medium ones. The highest party and state officials Vlada Stambuk, Radovan Bozovic, and Nebojsa Miljkovic were informed about that investment of the USA into Serbia in the amount of 70 billion dollars.

The central directorate of *KPMG* was the most powerful institution in Washington after the White House. It gave the main estimations and guarantees for all big business activities in the world. The *KPMG* trust decided in which activity money and pro it would be secure and in which that wouldn't be the case. The *KPMG* company, for instance, assessed the tobacco factory in Nis as one of the best in the Balkans and recommended it for mandatory purchasing and privatization. Why was that? Because the factory in Nis had huge amounts of high-quality tobacco from Vranje and Macedonia and could produce Marlboro Light with the US stamp. The pro it would be made on a cheap labor, low production cost in Nis, and high sales price in the USA and the world. That was the business that would take Serbia out of the economic mud.

During 1992, Dr Daniel Shein from Vienna mediated in the establishment of direct business cooperation between Peat Marwick, the representative of the *KPMG* concern from the USA and the people from the Government of Serbia on the reform of the Serbian economy and its privatization. The Government of Serbia accepted this initiative and negotiations with the representatives of *KPMG*, one of the world's largest corporations, which was the personification of economic and political power of the USA. I have in my possession the documentation on the cooperation between *KPMG* and the Government of Serbia on the reform and privatization of the Serbian economy and society, where it can be clearly seen what the transition plan was offered to Serbia by the USA.

After the meetings in Belgrade that lasted from 17th to 19th March 1992 and after the discussions on the program of the economic reform and privatization with the Government of Serbia and the

Vice President Nebojsa Maljkovic, *KPMG* and its representative Peat Marwick created a special program on 24th March regarding the tasks for the Government of Serbia. This program contained five projects:
- public debt management and macro-economic politics,
- negotiations with international development institutions,
- privatization, commercialization, and restructuring of large state companies,
- reform of financial institutions and obtaining investments, and
- establishment of an export and development bank.

The program was made on 31st March 1992 with the aim of promoting the sustainable development of the Republic of Serbia and assisting the Government of Serbia in achieving trust in the international financial circles in the world. Peat Marwick's team was supposed to help the Government of Serbia in the creation of the sustainable state budget, public debt management politics, and efficient state administration.

The team would also work on the new agreement with the IMF and the World Bank on the loans for structural harmonization and stabilization of the economy, for the support in the privatization, and the implementation of new financial mechanisms for the promotion of export and import of Serbia. The Americans offered Serbia the support of the European Community and the World Bank in this process. They suggested the forming of a local branch of the KPMG corporation, whose representative Lior Samuelson would become a business partner of the Government of Serbia.

The *KPMG* program of the economic reform and privatization was submitted to the Government of Serbia on 1st April 1992. It thoroughly described the process of the program realization in Serbia, which would be managed by six experts from Washington. In its most interesting part, on the matter of privatization, this program, as proposed, needed to achieve the following aims:

- the encouragement of efficiency and compatibility of medium and large state and public companies through restructuring, ownership transfer, and the private sector control, the attraction of foreign investments because of the financial capital, technology transfer, management staff, and new market,

- the mobilization of the public support to the Government of Serbia and its privatization program through communication with interest groups and media,
- the upgrade of the analytical education of the members of the Government of Serbia and private advisors for working on the KPMG privatization program, and
- the establishment of small non-bureaucratic offices for the on-field privatization which would conduct the assessment of companies and their ownership transformation.

At the *KPMG* suggestion, the Government of Serbia should form its team of employees that would work with Peat Marwick's team that, as the advisor of Serbian Government, was entitled to the income of 2% of the value of the conducted transitions and privatizations.

For the first year of work, the estimated costs of the two teams amounted to 2.4 billion dollars. The funds for their work would be provided by the USA, European Commission, the IMF, the World Bank, and the European Bank.

Unfortunately for the Serbs, Slobodan Milosevic and the Government of Serbia didn't accept the realization of the Program of the Economic Reform and Privatization offered by the *KPMG* trust, i.e. by the official Washington. Because of that rejection to transform and modernize with the US assistance, on 1st May 1992, the USA punished Serbs and Serbia by imposing international sanctions. With this embargo, Slobodan Milosevic pushed his own Serbian people and Serbian state downhill.

It is clear to me now that Milosevic wasn't aware that the real American message on the reform and privatization was: let us have the FRY to manage it and to organize it into a modern capitalist country. Milosevic thought that the USA would overthrow him and take his power if he handed over the Serbian and Yugoslav economy, and public and state capital to their experts. At the same time, he thought he was indestructible because he had behind him rebellious, anti-American people and police, as well as the YNA. He was spiteful to the USA to the furthest limits and defeated himself, his country and his people.

My conclusion today is simple: Slobodan Milosevic didn't know how to handle politics. He dealt solely with his power. Refusing the transition under the command of the USA, the

Serbian archon refused the changes and reforms of the country and society. The USA appreciated Serbia as the most perspective and the most advanced country of the Eastern Europe. The aim of the USA was to initiate the transition of the communist property and order in Serbia, as an example to other countries, and to form in Belgrade the first capitalist country among the former communist states. The USA and the West would invest hundreds of billions of dollars so that their companies could win the market of Serbia and former Yugoslavia and, then, enter the other countries of the former Soviet bloc.

When that was refused to be done in a peaceful manner, the West made itself a market in Serbia by force. Serbia was bombarded in order to destroy the Serbian economy and to violently turn the country into the market of capital and goods from the West. Kosovo was wrested to punish Slobodan Milosevic by losing his power and the Serbian people were punished, as well, for supporting their archon.

SELFISH SLOBA, TUDJMAN, AND ALIJA

When Slobodan Milosevic decided to refuse the American offer, by which he actually approved the introduction of sanctions, I tried to seek the help for the salvation of Yugoslavia and Serbia with the new Prime

Minister Milan Panic. On 19th August 1992, I sent a letter to the Yugoslav Prime Minister Milan Panic with the proposal for us to be a link between Washington and Belgrade, between the businessmen of the two countries, to the mutual benefit:

"I have been in Belgrade for the last two years and I have been trying to identify the main issues the solving of which I could help in, with the assistance of my friends from Washington and Europe. One of the steps proposed to me was the privatization I organized with the *KPMG* company – the Washington of ice, but, as you know, it is hard to do anything without the Government being involved. If Yugoslavia signs the agreement with *KPMG*, I could activate a very powerful PR machinery they have, including a quite serious possibility of cancelling the embargo. We can discuss that. In a separate envelope, I am sending you the agreement *KPMG* signed before the embargo and the letter on the intentions of Mr. Maljkovic, the Deputy Prime Minister. Mr. Slobodan Milosevic is aware of this. I do not know the reason why this program wouldn't be implemented in the entire Yugoslavia and give you a powerful argument against the foreign press. There are many programs I have started here, in which I use the US businessmen and politicians speaking to our benefit, but, as I have said, I need the official channels."

I suggested to Panic to meet up and realize the agreement with *KPMG*. He never replied to me. Milan Panic, an American citizen with the partisan biography, a millionaire that became a politician, and an even richer man in Belgrade, conducted his own private privatization. He had his own drug factory in Serbia producing medicines for mass sales to the Russians and the Chinese. He also had the ruling throne of the Prime Minister, even though he wasn't completely politically supported by either the USA or the Serbs.

The relations between the Serbian President Milosevic and the Yugoslav Prime Minister Panic were quite bad. A stalemate position occurred, which the Yugoslav President Dobrica Ćosic, persuaded by me, tried to resolve by using the Constitution of the FRY, but also the army of the FRY. Dobrica didn't reconcile Milosevic and Panic. Ćosic was too much of a softy and he didn't know how to do his presidential work. He was a pain in the neck to the conflicting President of Serbia and the Prime Minister of Yugoslavia.

I sent the letter of the similar contents as the one to Milan Panic to the Government of Serbia, hoping that someone in the Serbian authority would react and prevent the devastating consequences of the embargo imposed on us. The Government of Serbia didn't reply to my appeal either.

When I saw that sanctions were going to destroy the SFRY, but also my business in Belgrade, I tried to re-initiate the process of transition in Serbia through President George Bush Senior. I lived on both of the sides of the world and I could, as an observer in a game of chess, see and predict the moves of both of the sides, the USA and the SFRY. I tried to be neutral and assist both the USA and Serbia, but the tremendously bad player in Serbia, Slobodan Milosevic, prevented me from doing so.

Milosevic, Izetbegovic, and Tudjman

At the time, I didn't realize that Serbian leaders in Belgrade, Milosevic, Panic, and Ćosic, didn't even want what was the best for the Serbian people, but what was the best for them personally. And, they succeeded in that. Serbian people didn't protest much because they had no other alternative and because the Serbs loved living with misery and suffering.

And, while Franjo Tuđman, with the help of the USA, brought the Croatians from diaspora to assist him in the privatization of the state companies and in the fight for independent Croatia, Milosevic rejected the Serbian diaspora and created a new communist party with his wife Mira, JUL (the Yugoslav Left). In that way he wanted to fulfill the dream of his wife, Mirjana Markovic, to officially become the successor of Josip Broz Tito and to rule together in the incomplete Yugoslavia – as new Tito and Jovanka.

Milosevic used nationalism as a means of acquiring power in Serbia. He used the misfortunes of Kosmet Serbs, abolished the autonomy of Kosmet and Vojvodina, and put under his control the presidency of Yugoslavia and the YNA, and thus inaugurated Serbia as the dominant power in Yugoslavia.

The close bond between and the mixture of communism and nationalism defined the roles played by certain individuals on the positions of power, such was Slobodan Milosevic in Serbia, Franjo Tuđman in Croatia, and Alija Izetbegovic in Bosnia and Herzegovina.

Partially as a response to the moves of Milosevic towards the centralization of Serbia and the dominance over the SFRY, and partially of their own accord, nationalists came to power in other republics, as well. Franjo Tuđman, the former general of the YNA and the head of the Croatian Democratic Community, gathered the nationalists in Croatia and became its first president. He was well-known for writing the revisionist review of the actions of Ustashas during the Second World War, which reduced the scope of the crimes the NDH (Independent State of Croatia) committed against the Serbs and, thus, spread the Serbian nationalistic fire.

In Bosnia and Herzegovina, Alija Izetbegovic came to power as the leader of the Muslim Party of Democratic Action. He had been imprisoned during Tito's rule for writing *The Islamic Declaration*, a document that was broadly interpreted to advocate for the establishment of a Muslim religious country inside Bosnia.

The Bosnian Serbs used the past of Izetbegovic to present themselves as the fighters at the first line of Europe's defense against the intrusion of Islam into the Old Continent and to show how important it is for them to live in a separate state, not together with the Bosnian Muslims.

Those people, together with Milosevic, Tuđman, and Izetbegovic, to a different extent, manipulated nationalism in order to gain financial capital and political power and retain their rule. Therefore, they should carry the heaviest burden of responsibility for the disintegration of the SFRY and persecution and death of thousands of people.

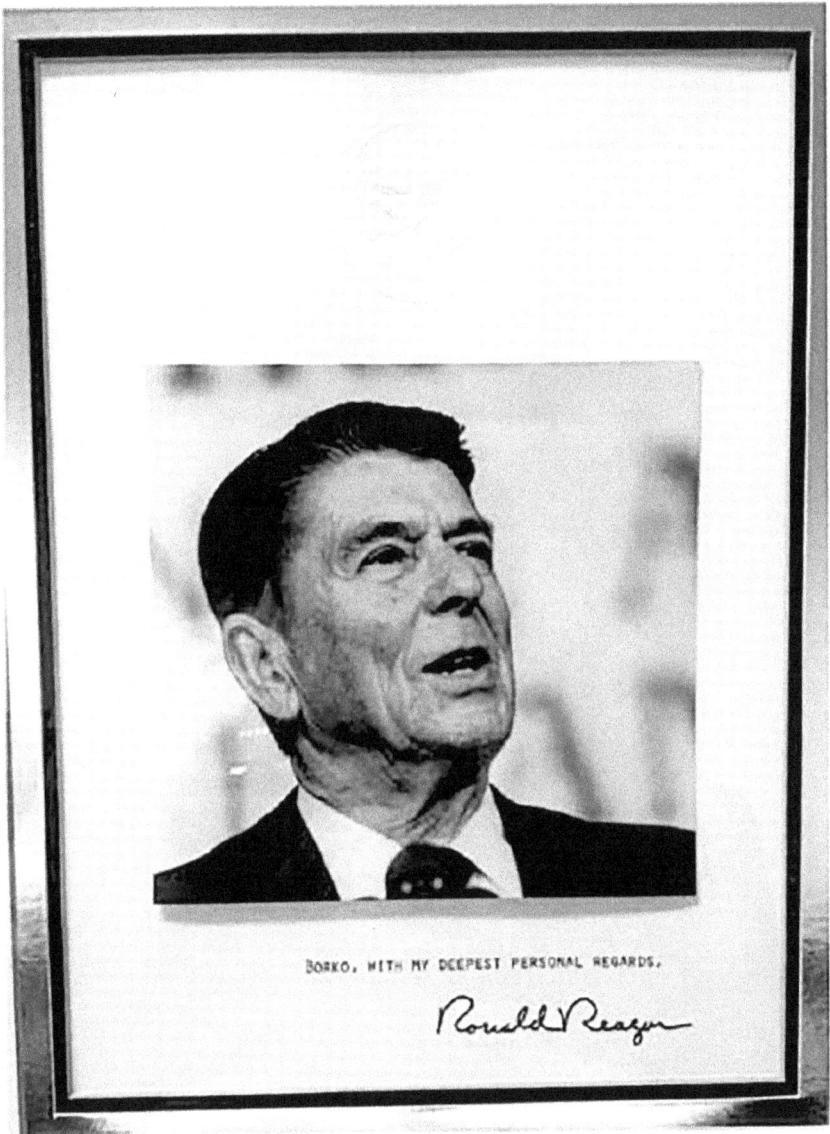

BORKO, WITH MY DEEPEST PERSONAL REGARDS,

Ronald Reagan

US President Ronald Reagan awarded Dr Borko Djordjevic

MIRA BANISHES THE AMERICANS

Mira Markovic, Milosevic's wife and the head of the Yugoslav Left, the second most powerful leader of Serbia, expressed a nervous and dangerous intolerance of foreigners, particularly the Americans. When US *Texaco* and *Shell* wanted to buy the company *Jugopetrol*, Mira Markovic personally didn't allow that. That was probably because she would lose her sycophants, the directors of this company who brought her fur, scarves, and other expensive gifts.

To be specific, even though sanctions were imposed on the third Yugoslavia by the decision of the international community in May 1992, the Americans and other Westerners constantly continued persuading Milosevic and his wife Mira to conduct the transition of ownership relations and replace communism with capitalism. They continuously, but covertly, though sometimes even publicly, refused that.

Mirjana Mira Markovic PhD

When I brought around a dozen of US congressmen, senators, and owners of multinational companies to Serbia and Belgrade to see the situation and enter the process of privatization of our economy, I introduced them to the rulers from the Milosevic family. *Philip Morris* Company, the management of which my mother-in-law was a member of, wanted to buy Nis Tobacco Industry. It was an investment of around 200 million dollars. Slobodan Milosevic didn't allow that. His wife Mirjana Markovic rejected the offer of the Italian company Septa for the privatization in Serbia. General Jovo Popovic managed all Mira Markovic's affairs. With the help of two men named Dragan Tomic, the Director of *Jugopetrol* and the director of *Simpo*, the general financed *Radio Kosava*, which was run by her daughter Marija Milosevic. The private entertainment of the Serbian archon's daughter was financed with Serbian people's money.

I mediated in one business activity between the French and Jovo Popovic and, as the general failed to pay them, they charged me for the loss of as much as 800,000 Deutsche marks. They didn't know that, because of general Popovic, I lost a red Volkswagen Golf which someone from his crew had stolen and resold.

The director Miodrag Jaksic didn't want the PTT of Serbia to get privatized. In 1994, I brought him *Motorola Company* to Serbia to introduce mobile telephony. It was before Zoran Markovic from Canada did that, and later Bogoljub Karic in Belgrade, as well. The Milosevic family rejected *Motorola* and started mobile telephony business with some fraudsters from the USA.

Sony Company, at the peak of their power, wanted to buy *El Nis* company:

"No way! You're not offering enough money."

That was the answer of Mira Markovic and Milosevic's Yugoslavia, because he was afraid he would lose power if foreign companies entered the country. Local party managers in Nis feared Sony would take their power and authority.

I suggested Buca Prohaska from the SPS that we should initiate a campaign and explain the people the need to conduct political changes, privatization, and democratization and to win over voters for Milosevic in that manner.

"Are you out of your mind? People don't want to renounce their self-governing position and ownership over the state companies," Prohaska told me.

Then I realized that the control of the Yugoslav people and property are the key of Slobodan Milosevic's power. That is why Milosevic didn't accept the economic transition and the change of ownership over the state property, because, in that case, he wouldn't be able to control the people through the directors and companies and have the power. In Serbia, there were no independent businessmen or companies, as in Slovenia, who would conduct the transition in spite of Milosevic.

Slobodan Milosevic also rejected doing business with the five largest US companies, some of them being *Westinghouse, Honeywell,* and *General Electric.* He behaved like a mobster and racketeer because he wanted the US companies to pay him in cash for working in the FRY and Serbia.

The USA showed their good will and offered Milosevic to lift sanctions off Yugoslavia and Serbia if he allowed the US capital and companies to enter the state companies and Yugoslav market. Such an offer was on the table of each future Prime Minister of Serbia.

"The boss has forbidden and stopped it all," Vlada Stambuk, a con idant of Slobodan Milosevic, told me.

"Which boss? Slobodan Milosevic or Mira Markovic?" I asked my friend Vlada Stambuk.

"Well, Milosevic," Stambuk was trying to persuade me, although I thought it was all the doing of the communist heroine Dr Mirjana Markovic.

With Slobodan Milosevic and Mira Markovic rejecting all those American offers, the tedious sanctions intensi ied. Many Serbian officials and even citizens were forbidden from entering the USA. The list of the undesirable ones included all the members of the Milosevic family and all his communist directors. I left Serbia then, at the end of 1997, and went to the USA.

ASSASSINATE BORKO THE SPY

Slobodan Milosevic knew that I, Borko Djordjevic, the worldly doctor, as his lot used to gossip about me, was Radovan Karadzic's man, and "an American spy and traitor". He browsed through my file, which he'd obtained from the State Security of Serbia (RDB) and he deleted the information that I'd completed post-academic doctoral studies in medicine in Belgrade in 1994, though he requested for my doctorate to be checked at the Faculty of Medicine in Belgrade. To be specific, Slobodan Milosevic took my work resume from Dr Grbic, PhD, the Dean of the Faculty of Medicine and my party résumé from the League of Communists of Yugoslavia (SKJ) and he made a secret file. He, who had been a close associate to the Americans for a while, declared me, Dr Djordjevic, PhD, an American spy.

Borko Djordjevic with Americans visiting Radovan Karadzic

Borko B. Djordjevic, PhD in Medicine in 1995

Since 1995, when Milosevic labeled me as his enemy, whenever I would enter or leave Serbia, I was particularly checked or detained for hearing by the police. As I was always carrying all the documents and notes on my correspondence with the former US President Jimmy Carter, and a photo with him, Milosevic's policemen confiscated those documents on one occasion.

Milosevic personally launched a police hunt after me, because he believed I'd deceived and betrayed him. Sloba ordered his police officers and criminals to assassinate me. There was a bounty of 400,000 dollars for my head. Tomislav Pejovic, the sculptor of Tito's busts and an intimate friend of Jovanka Broz tipped me that a criminal nicknamed Pomorandza had decided to assassinate me and earn 400,000 dollars. I hired a bodyguard to protect me, but he asked 400,000 to save my life from that Milosevic's assassin. I refused to pay for such protection. That wasn't enough to Milosevic, so he ordered Radovan Karadzic to kill me:

"Dr Borko is an American spy and a traitor of the Serbian people. Get rid of him!"

Karadzic didn't get rid of me, but he left me to my fate, to deal with the Milosevic family on my own.

The life, however, wanted me to meet the entire Milosevic family during the time of that hunt. The son, Marko Milosevic, got injured in a car race. He had a spine injury and stayed in the Military Medical Academy (VMA) at the ward on the 13th floor. I did some work at VMA and met Milosevic's son at the time and shook hands with him. "Little Marko", as he was called at the time, felt the need to get me acquainted with his viewpoint of the situation in Yugoslavia:

"This is a disaster. You cannot make head or tail of this situation. The Communism has lapsed and it's the time of Capitalism. That's what we should be fighting for," Marko Milosevic was saying at the time when his parents were trying to save their Communism from downfall.

In the late nineties, it was evident that "Little Marko" was a danger to society and everyone surrounding him because he was carrying guns and automatic weapons and threatening journalists and everyone else he disliked.

Marija Milosevic walked around Belgrade with her boyfriend from the RDB, who, being a secret agent, always carried two guns. Marija often enjoyed shooting from those guns in public places. She organized midnight parties in the villas of Dedinje where she demonstrated her cowboy and gunman abilities.

I also met Milosevic's wife, professor Mira Markovic. She told me she wanted to "do her stomach and thighs", but in a nice way, by liposuction. Mira had been operated by a Greek doctor. He removed the fat from her stomach, but he left her skin sagging like a curtain. She asked me to tighten that skin and her thighs. I replied that it was done best with a scalpel and that I could nip and tuck her. She smoothly refused my offer, which was exactly what I'd wanted. The fact is, I didn't want to risk my life for five kilos of fat on the stomach of the wife of Slobodan Milosevic, the most powerful and dangerous woman in Serbia during the 1990s. I could see that for myself.

I sold a house in Dedinje for 700,000 Swiss francs. The buyer was, allegedly, a policeman called Zika. A few days later, three men kidnapped me and held me in a basement of a house for three days. The man with hoarse voice, who said he was a war veteran, shouted at me, put a pistol tube in my mouth, and threatened:

"I will kill you if you don't give me money. I have a throat cancer and I'm dying anyway. I have nothing to lose. And, you will live if you pay up."

I paid my kidnapper 200,000 marks and he released me. I later found out that the kidnapping had been conducted by the people of Mira Markovic from the Yugoslav Left and some supporters of hers from *Duga* company.

SLOBA'S COCK

Slobodan Milosevic was a milksop around his wife Mira. He spoke quietly and cautiously so that his wife wouldn't hear. Mira Markovic was a secret ruler of the FRY and Serbia. She imagined she was a daughter of Josip Broz and that she was supposed to be an heiress to Tito's Yugoslavia.

She'd grown up on the Brijuni Islands among the members of the Yugoslav Communist elite and she wanted to be, if not Tito, then the second Jovanka Broz. That was many times clearly stated in her political actions and her letters and books. Slobodan Milosevic intimately shared that fantasy of Mira Markovic and supported her in her aspiration for the two of them to become new Tito and Jovanka.

The recipe of their political career Mira Markovic once summed into two words: money and political power. She confessed she organized the life of Slobodan Milosevic so that he would go where he would have power, but also money. Thus, Sloba worked in *Tehnogas*, which was loaded with money, and then in *Beobanka*, which he stepped out of and took the power of his best friend, Ivan Stambolic. After that, Milosevic turned the entire Serbia into his personal and private bank.

How dangerous Dr Mira Markovic was can be seen from this dialogue we had in 1997 in a hotel, over lunch I'd been invited to by the head of security of the then director of JUL, who was dating Marija Milosevic. He was carrying two pistols behind his belt and bragging about overthrowing Milosevic:

"His picture fell off the closed while Marija and I were kissing!"

He suddenly asked me in confidence:

"Doctor, do you have anything for Mira's husband? His cock won't go up. Is there a cure for that?"

I understood this question on the penis of Mira's husband, Slobodan Milosevic, as a serious provocation and the opportunity for Mira Markovic - if I provided any answer, it would be turned into a rumor that allegedly I, Dr Djordjevic, was disseminating around Belgrade, saying that Sloba's dick can't erect. And, it was also the opportunity to lose my head for that.

I took the first chance I had to run away to the USA to avoid getting a stick or a cudgel over the head as a side dish to Mira Markovic's sweet carrots.

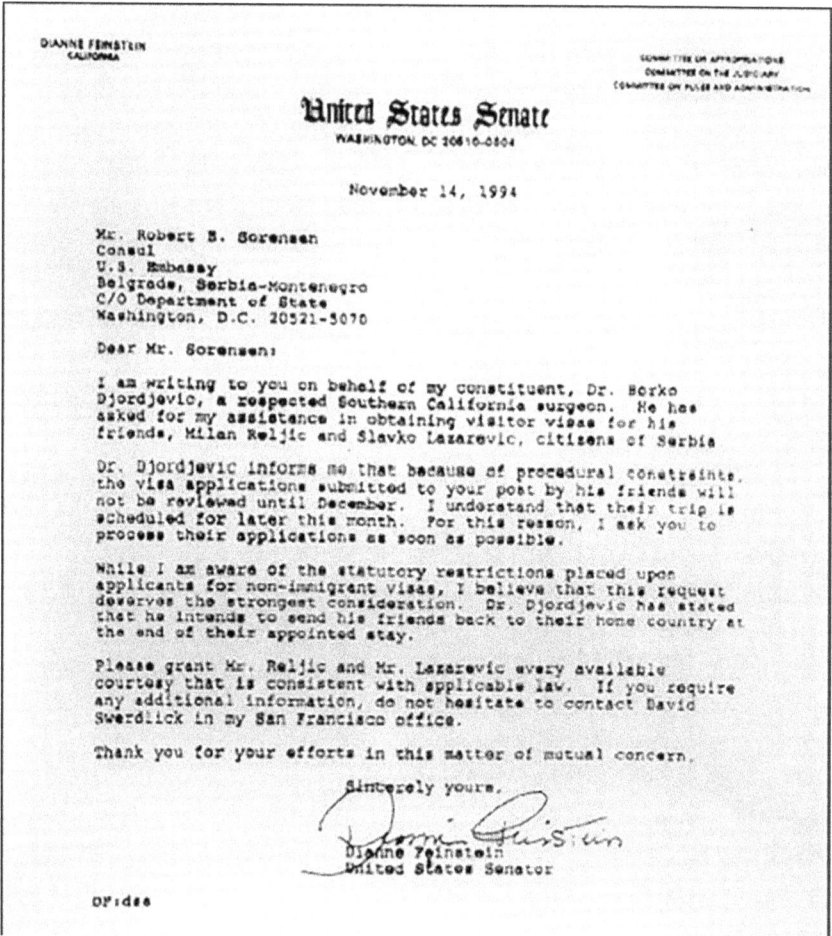

The letter of Dr Djordjevic to the US Senate on the visit of Serbian citizens to the USA

SLOBODAN MILOSEVIC'S DAUGHTER-IN-LAW

Of all the members of the Milosevic family, I had the best cooperation with Sloba's daughter-in-law, Milica Gajic. She phoned me at the beginning of 1996.

"Dr Djordjevic, I saw you on television. You were in a show together with Ruska Mulina and you talked about the beautifying of women's breasts. And, my mum's hairdresser also told me that you could provide some medical assistance to me."

"What's the matter?"

"I have a problem with my nose and breathing."

Milica Gajic from Pozarevac was just nineteen. She was a girlfriend and, later, the common-law wife of Marko Milosevic, the son of the Serbian archon, Slobodan.

I received her in my clinic in Igalo and opened a medical record for her.

"I was born on 24th February 1977 in Pozarevac, where my parents, father Rajko and mother Mirjana, live, together with my brother Milan. I'm a student," she said.

Milica Gajic as a patient in 1996

I could conclude from her voice that this girl feared the surgery, but she wasn't upset, which gave me the opportunity to conclude that she was a stable person determined to undergo the surgery.

Milica Gajic came to my clinic because she was having difficulties with breathing and breast hypotrophy. They were tiny, like a half of a grapefruit. She came to Igalo alone, which was supposed to mean that the girlfriend of Marko Milosevic had decided to cure and beautify without her family and Serbian public knowing about that.

My Mediterranean Surgical Center in Igalo was the first private hospital for plastic surgery in Montenegro. I bought a part of "Simo Milosevic" Institute, the left wing of it, two thousand square meters in size, and turned it into a clinic. In it, during the war in the SFRY in the '90s, I treated children injured in armed conflicts in Bosnia and Herzegovina and Montenegro.

When the war abated after the Dayton Agreement in 1995, the Mediterranean Surgical Center in Igalo started operating normally. On the 2nd February 1996, when I received Milica Gajic, I performed a medical checkup and had a conversation with her.

"What is your general health like?"

"Fine," Milica Gajic replied.

"Have you had any major health issues?"

"No."

"What has your appetite been like in the recent years?"

"Decreased."

"What about your weight?"

"The same."

"Do you often feel thirsty?"

"No."

"Do you feel you have less energy?"

"No."

"Do you have problems sleeping?"

"No."

"Do you do any recreational activities?"

"A little."

"Do you smoke?"

"Yes."

"How many cigarettes a day?"

"Twenty."

"Do you take any alcohol?"

"No."

"Have you ever had a surgery before?"

"Yes, my tonsils when I was five."

The physical examination showed that Milica Gajic had been infected with mumps as a child, but that she was healthy at the time. She was a young woman of medium-built, good osteo-muscular structure, conscious, oriented, and afebrile. Her skin had a normal color. The sound of her lungs was normal, her hearth rhythmic and without any noise. She left the impression of being a mentally stable person. This medical report was signed by the physician Vlasta Bozovic.

Milica Gajic was photographed before and after the surgery. She gave a written consent for that, as well as the consent to use her medical record in public.

The surgery of Milica Gajic lasted from 9.35 to 11.20. Her nose was corrected, and breasts augmented. Milica Gajic was transferred from the operating room to the hospital room at 7 p.m. She was mildly upset during the night. On the 5th February, the surgical drains were removed, and she was upset then as well. She feared how she would look to herself after the surgery. She was satisfied.

The girlfriend of Marko Milosevic received therapy and was quickly recovering. She signed the request for the early discharge off the clinic, because she wanted to go to Belgrade and see Marko. That wasn't common in my medical practice, but I couldn't refuse the daughter-in-law of Slobodan Milosevic, the President of Serbia and the FRY. She was a very good patient and a kind person.

Her discharge list from the Mediterranean Surgical Center in Igalo was sent to Dr Dragan Ivanovic at the Military Medical Academy in Belgrade. The following day, on 6th February 1996, the patient Milica Gajic was also sent to Belgrade with a cast on her nose. However, several days later, Milica Gajic called me from the VMA in Belgrade to come and personally remove the cast off her nose. She looked nice and was very satisfied. I couldn't take a photo of her in Belgrade because at VMA, next to her, there was her boyfriend, her common-law husband, Marko Milosevic, the son of Slobodan Milosevic.

Marko Milosevic and Milica Gajic

I didn't see my patient, Milica Gajic, for many years after that. During her marriage with Marko Milosevic, she gave birth to a son, who was named Marko. When, in 2002, the son of Slobodan Milosevic escaped to Russia, his wife Milica and their son Marko remained in Pozarevac. She started working at *Megatrend University* in Pozarevac. Marko Milosevic got married in Russia and got a daughter, as Serbian media reported. In 2014, Milica Gajic showed her photos on *Facebook* from a beach in Egypt, where her beautiful breasts that I had made could be seen.

NEW TITO

The biographies of Slobodan Milosevic and his wife, Mirjana Markovic, speak enough about them being rather unhappy and traumatized people. Sloba was born in 1941 in a family in Pozarevac. His father, Svetozar, was a priest and his mother, Stanislava, a housewife. His father left him, when he was little. Svetozar Milosevic committed a suicide from a gun in 1962, and his mother, Stanislava, hanged herself in 1974.

Slobodan Milosevic with his parents: father Svetozar and mother Stanislava

In 1965, Slobodan got married to a childhood friend from Pozarevac, Mirjana Markovic. She was also raised without parents. She was born in 1942. Her mother, Vera Miletic was killed in the war, and her father, Moma Markovic, neglected her for his party and state obligations. She was raised by her grandparents.

Both of them grew up to be egoistic, without any sense of love and care for close people. They brought up their children, Marija and Marko, to be independent, but also disdainful.

Both Sloba and Mira built their business and political career with the help of their house friend, Ivica Stambolic, who Slobodan worked with in *Tehnogas* company. With his assistance, Mira got the job as a professor of sociology at the University of Belgrade.

Being a law graduate, Milosevic continued his career in banking. For the first two years he was the official representative of Beobanka in New York. From there, he brought back home the story that he was "an American man" and that he had strong connections in Washington.

He was a Communist from 1959 to 1990, when the League of Communists of Yugoslavia was turned into the Socialist Party of Serbia, according to his orders. When he replaced Ivica Stambolic from the position of the first person of the League of Communists of Serbia in 1986, he became the president of the Central Committee of the League of Communists of Serbia.

From 1989 to 1991, he was the Chairman of the Presidency of Serbia, from January 1991 to 1997, the President of Serbia, and finally, the President of the FRY from 7th October 2000.

Slobodan Milosevic was the official ruler, but his wife Mirjana Markovic ruled from the shadow. As rulers, they lived in the official Tito's villa. Their children, son Marko and daughter Marija, didn't want to live with them.

Milosevic and Mira were accompanied by the party and state entourage who waited for crumbs of their personal and political power to fall on them. The part of the political power of the Milosevic family was shared by the hairdresser of Mrs Mirjana, an experienced hair care master, Snezana Radosevic. She lived in Zemun and had a hairdressing salon in the center of Belgrade, in Cika Ljubina Street. She bragged to me, while she was my patient, that apart from Mirjana Markovic and Slobodan Milosevic, she was the hairdresser of their daughter-in-law,

Milica, and the Professor Radmila Milentijevic from the USA, who became a Minister.

The malicious people reproached Snezana Radosevic for being friends with the members of the Milosevic family. Some even gossiped about the hairdresser of Mirjana Markovic and Slobodan Milosevic saying that, thanks to them, she had got 500,000 marks from Beobanka. It is still not clear whether they were a loan or a non-refundable gift.

One of the people of Slobodan Milosevic was a businessman and a fat cat, Bogoljub Karic, the younger brother in the well-known Karic family and Braća Karic company. Bogoljub, Dragomir, Sreten, and Zoran are the four sons of Danica and Janicije Karic from Peć, who managed to become celebrities in Serbia. Partly because of their entrepreneurship and building factories in poor Kosovo and Metohija, and more because of the support of the Serbian President Slobodan Milosevic, the Karic brothers built an empire. And, Bogoljub Karic had an ambition to become the President of Serbia, because of which he ended up in front of the court and got removed from the public life.

I performed an operation on his parents Janicije and Danica Karic in 1988. I removed lesions from their faces. They were wonderful patients.

There are countless theories on how Milosevic actually helped the Karic family and how they helped him, but, to date, the Karic family remained persistent in their claim that they had been "in good relations with everyone", as well as that, as Bogoljub put it, "power can bend anyone, as a pig in a pan, and roast them in the oven".

In the oven or without it, the Karic family left the infamous "years of denouement" with millions the number of which is unknown, with companies dealing with all imaginable and unimaginable activities, and with property all over the world.

The personal physician of Milosevic, Professor Doctor Radosav Dragojevic bragged that he treated two greatest Serbian rulers from diabetes – Tito and Mira. He was present when Tito died of diabetes. He had personally known Milosevic for quite a long time. He checked his health and spoke to him about Tito.

Slobodan Milosevic was a stupid politician, without any tact and without the sense of diplomacy, and compromise. Stubborn and single-minded as he was, he just pushed his intentions forward. I have no idea why he believed he could defeat the west and become Tito. Tito created the Communist Yugoslavia, and Sloba tore it apart.

Tito minimized Serbia within Yugoslavia and Sloba, raising it within the SFRY, completely destroyed the Republic of Serbia. Tito made Yugoslavia into the Third World leader and a strong non-aligned country and Milosevic made Serbia a loser and the defeated culprit that caused war and calamity.

Tito was the world leader number three, and Sloba was the "Butcher of the Balkans" number one. Tito made the Yugoslavs a world-known and popular nation, and Sloba made Serbs a criminal nation.

Tito promoted the cult of war and the labor class selfgoverning. Sloba promoted the cult of protests and street riots, which emptied the work halls and companies. Workers and citizens rallied to support Sloba and, on that foundation, he built his selfish rule without the labor class.

Tito built the state on the US loans and democratized the country and Milosevic deceived the Americans, didn't take their money, and pushed the country into a ghetto. Tito developed foreign policy and trade, and Sloba contributed to the imposing of sanctions and isolation of Serbia.

Tito allowed the development of private property and self-governing capitalism. Milosevic rejected the transition of state ownership into private and the privatization of state companies, but he allowed the creation of tycoons, i.e. private fat cats that performed the privatization of companies to the benefit of the Milosevic family, SPS, and JUL. SPS unlawfully took all the property of the League of Communists of Serbia and the League of Communists of Yugoslavia, as well as of the municipal committees and assigned it to themselves.

Tito's children and grandchildren were not a part of state and social elite, and Sloba's children were privileged private businessmen that got rich on doing business with the national money and state property. Tito's children lived in his country, Milosevic's children ran away from Serbia, his son to Russia, and his daughter to Montenegro, because their father had destroyed Serbia and left it to his political successors in a miserable state.

AMERICAN YUGOSLAVIA

Modern Yugoslavia, created after the Second World War, existed for forty- ive years as a federation of six republics. In Slovenia, Croatia, Bosnia and Herzegovina, Serbia, Montenegro, Macedonia, as well as in Kosmet, and in Vojvodina, people of ten different nationalities lived relatively peacefully. Serbs, with 36%, comprised the majority of that population. They lived in Serbia, in Vojvodina Province, in Montenegro, and in the Province of Kosovo and Metohija. Croats with almost 20%and Muslims with nearly 10% were the second and the third nation of the SFRY, respectively. Almost 3% of the population declared as Yugoslavs.

Being half a Slovenian and half a Croat, some even claim he was a Jew with Polish origin, Josip Broz Tito, the president for life of that country, carefully structured the federal government and the League of Communists of Yugoslavia, i.e. the executive and political power, in order to ensure that no ethnic group can dominate in politics.

After 1945, Tito made the residents of the most southern Republic of Macedonia into a Macedonian nation, and he of icially formalized Muslims as a constituent nation of Yugoslavia. It was Broz's attempt to establish mutual balance of ethnic groups and to confront Serbian domination.

In their day-to-day life and practice, most Muslims didn't signi icantly differ from their Serbian and Croatian neighbors. They spoke the same language, ate the same food, and mostly led worldly lives. The not so numerous Muslim population in Bosnia and Herzegovina was spread around the republic. The only areas with concentrated Muslim population were in the far north-western part of the republic, near Bihać and several small places in the east of Bosnia.

Josip Broz Tito visiting Richard Nixon in Washington

During the Second World War, Serbs, Croats, and Muslims waged a brutal civil war, in which Croats and some Muslims were in an alliance with Germany and Axis Powers, while most Serbs were in an alliance with the West and East Allies.

Since both the irst Kingdom of Yugoslavia and the second Communist Yugoslavia were on the crossroads of the west Christianity, Orthodoxy, and Islam, some political analysts claimed that these three religions and civilizations could not voluntarily coexist for a long time and that, due to ierce external in luences of Catholicism, Orthodoxy, and Islam, they were destined to break up. The argument stating that those three civilizations were too different to function together, regardless of their long history of peaceful coliving, was often used by the leaders of nationalist parties, which took over the politics in Yugoslavia in the late '80s and early '90s, as the justi ication for the independence war of their entities.

The history of all the three Yugoslavias, the Kingdom, the Communist, and Milosevic's one, is closely connected with the diplomatic and political relations of Belgrade and Washington. It turned out that those relations during the rule of Josip Broz were crucial for the rapid development of the FNRY (Federative National Republic of Yugoslavia) and the SFRY into a modern socialist country and, during the rule of Slobodan Milosevic, they represented the doom of Yugoslavia. The political and diplomatic relations of Belgrade and

Washington started back in the 19th century at the initiative of the Principality of Serbia, because the Serbs wanted to sign their first trade agreement with the Americans. A young Member of Parliament, Nikola Pasic, talked about that in February 1882:

"The USA is a powerful country, both on land and sea, and it can be included into the greatest and most powerful countries. It has made agreements with France, England, Germany. Thus, whatever it could obtain from these powers, it has obtained it and, on the other hand, all other powers obtained from it everything they could. Can it, then, be suggested, gentlemen, that we, small and week Serbia, could obtain and take more from the USA than the other powers have obtained and taken?"

With the majority of votes, on 3rd February 1882, the National Parliament adopted the agreement, submitted by Prince Milan Obrenovic, and the convention on diplomatic relations. The US Senate, without any debates and amendments, adopted these two documents on 5th July 1882.

Meanwhile, the first American diplomat, Eugene Schuyler, was appointed Minister Plenipotentiary and General Consul in Romania, Serbia, and Greece. The first American Consulate was at 7 Francuska Street, at the address that would later become the seat of the Writers' Club. The first diplomatic representative of the USA in Belgrade, Ambassador Eugene Schuyler took of ice on 10th November 1882 by handing over a letter of credit to King Milan Obrenovic. Schuyler had previously participated in the final phase of the negotiations in the establishment of the consulate in Belgrade and the telegrams he was sending to Washington at the time could say a great deal of his farsightedness.

From the arrival of the first American diplomat in Belgrade to the First World War, our relations would be more influenced by the export of prunes worth one million dollars per year and the wonders of Nikola Tesla than the great politics. In the first years of the First World War, the USA was not mentioned in the war aims of Serbia. In November 1917, the USA decided to send Serbia a monthly aid of one million dollars. Then, a Serbian delegation travelled to the USA to seek support for the Macedonian Front and the unification of the South Slavs. The delegation was in the Congress when President Woodrow Wilson read his famous fourteen points on the post-war world order. In Point 11, he directly mentions Serbia demanding the occupier to evacuate its territory and to secure its access to the sea. The cooperation during the First World War was one of the brightest pages of the Serbian-American relations.

Until the beginning of the Second World War, the USA had its diplomatic envoys in Belgrade. The first one in the Kingdom of Serbs, Croats, and Slovenes was Henry Percival Dodge, from 1919 to 1926. Then, in the Kingdom of Yugoslavia, the envoy was John Daniel Prince, until 1932. Arthur Bliss Lane represented the USA from 1937 to 1941.

When, in December 1941, the USA officially became a participant in the Second World War, it supported the royal government in London and the Chetnik Movement of Draza Mihailovic in Serbia and Bosnia until 1944. During that period, the last diplomatic envoy of the USA was Anthony Drexel Biddle, who became the first Ambassador of the USA in Belgrade in 1943. He was succeeded by Lincoln MacVeagh, the US Ambassador in the liberated Belgrade in 1944.

During the war, the USA had a few military missions, i.e. a few intelligence officers in the area of Yugoslavia, particularly in two resistance movements. With the movement of Draza Mihailovic, Americans had two great missions. The first was led by the Colonel Albert Seitz and the head of the other was the Colonel Robert McDowell. In the other mission, which had the additional task to save the American pilots, who had participated in bombing missions and had been downed above Serbia, Romania, and Bulgaria, there was the Lieutenant Ellsworth Kramer.

Apart from the heads of the missions who left valuable reports on the state in Serbia, on the Partisan Movement led by Josip Broz Tito, and on the Chetnik Movement led by Draza

Mihailovic, the field reports of the missions' members sent to their bosses are also interesting. One of them is the report of Lieutenant Kramer.

After the victory in 1945, the USA supported Tito, who enrolled the FNRY into the membership of NATO. Between 1951 and 1971, we received 1.56 billion dollars of economic and around seventy million dollars of military aid.

"During the Cold War, Yugoslavia was a protected and sometimes pampered child of the American and western diplomacy," marked Warren Zimmermann, the US Ambassador in Belgrade at the end of '80s.

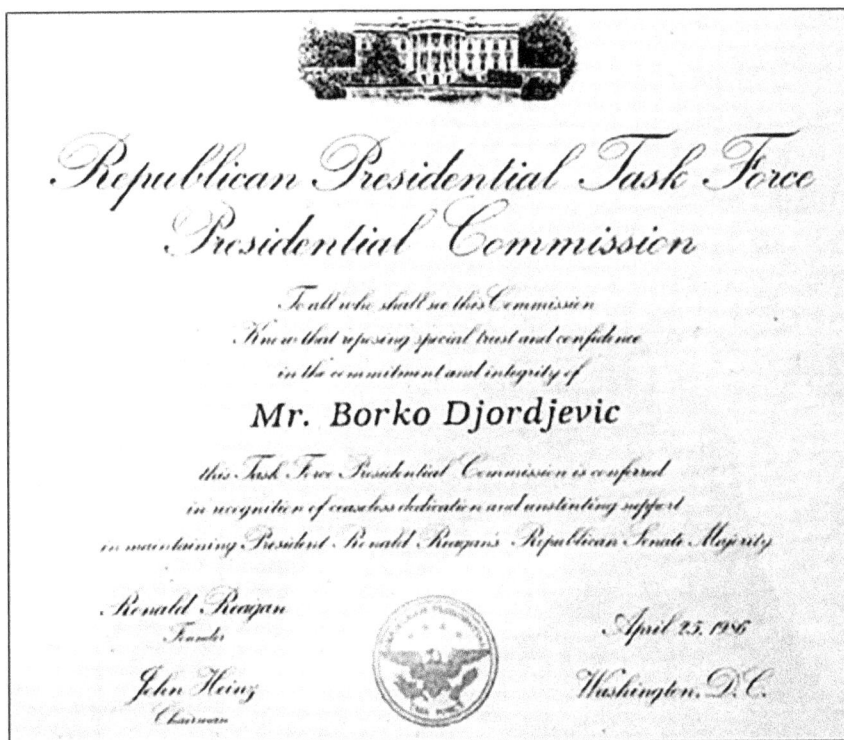

A US representative Dr. Borko Djordjevic, a member of the US Republican Party

POLITICIANS AND SPIES

However, the history has shown that the USA always sent to Yugoslavia, i.e. to Serbia and Belgrade, the ambassadors who had a negative disposition and who often behaved both as politicians and spies. Those were mostly the people who, with professional diplomacy, but also using intelligence, protected their network of friends and acquaintances in Belgrade and through them, or directly, exerted tough pressure on Yugoslav and Serbian authorities. Richard Stolz, the former Deputy Manager of the CIA in charge of foreign operations, wrote about that:

"In the '70s and '80s, we didn't pay much attention to the internal affairs of the former Yugoslavia. We observed the wider context, first of all the relation with the Soviet Union and the Warsaw Pact. Yugoslavia was essentially stable at the time and we were interested in the Cold-War developments. We were not so much focused on the events in Yugoslavia, as we maybe should have been."

Stolz was active during the Cold War and, according to him, the most relevant task at the time was to reveal the capabilities and intentions of the USSR and the Warsaw Pact. As one of the most significant secret operations, the former high official of the CIA emphasized the one in which a Polish colonel was delivering an enormous amount of information on the Warsaw Pact.

The Americans in former Yugoslavia had two diplomatic missions: the Embassy in Belgrade and the General Consulate in Zagreb. In our capital city, 35 out of around 70 American officials had the diplomatic status and immunity. There were also 220 Yugoslav citizens working there, most of whom on permanent contracts. In accordance with their political and diplomatic practice, the USA always sent to Yugoslavia the people educated about and familiar with the Eastern Europe, the Balkans, and Yugoslavia.

Before coming to Belgrade, many American diplomats would serve in Zagreb, at the Consulate. Thus, the Ambassadors Warren Zimmermann, William Montgomery, and Kyle Scott were in that Consulate. There are diplomatic experts that claim that, for American diplomats, Belgrade usually was the ticket to Moscow.

At the same time, that meant that the events in the Soviet Union could be best followed precisely from the SFRY.

The US Embassy was established in 1945 and, immediately, through its representatives, the USA organized the classic intelligence work, connecting with the remains of the disempowered parties and collaborators. According to the American regulations, the US Ambassador in a foreign country is, at the same time, the head of the American intelligence community that has sixteen secret services, but Serbs fear the CIA most.

However, some American Ambassadors didn't want to be the first spies of the USA in Yugoslavia, so they would leave the function of the secret services head to their deputies or secretaries. Some diplomats liked leading the CIA in Belgrade. Such were, for instance, Warren Zimmermann and William Montgomery.

The first head of the American mission in Yugoslavia after the Second World War was Harold Schoutz. He was appointed on 20th February 1946 and, as Dr Ranko Petrovic wrote, he had the title of the Charge d'Affaires. The new US Ambassador, Richard Peterson, arrived in Belgrade at the end of 1944 and stayed until the beginning of 1946, when he observed the Tito's trial of the General Draza Mihailovic.

In the mid-July 1947, he was replaced by Ambassador Cavendish W. Cannon. He was a witness to the Russian and Yugoslav Communist altercation and the political exile of Cominformists ("Ibeovci"). As the representative of the USA and its diplomacy, Ambassador Cannon had a hard task to initiate the Cold War in the Yugoslavian area, which he was in charge of till the end of January 1950.

He was replaced by Ambassador George V. Allen. His task was more humane; he took care of the delivery of the US aid, the famous Truman's eggs, which the Yugoslav Government didn't want to accept. Ambassador Allen advocated for and pioneered in the development of the US military aid to the FNRY, which was later actively continued to be developed by the new diplomatic representative of the USA. That was James W. Riddleberger who, according to the data of Professor Ranko Petrovic, the author of the studies on the US politics, took the of ice of the Ambassador on 16th November 1953. He was a witness to the Soviet rapprochement with Yugoslavia and the arrival of Nikita Khrushchev in an official visit to Josip Broz.

At the end of February 1958, the USA sent Karl Rankin to Belgrade. He was the observer at the First Conference of the Non-Aligned in 1961, after which Yugoslavia was marked as a country that was moving away from the USA and turning into an Anti-American factor in the Third World. In order to have a greater control over the official Belgrade, a wellknown Kremlin expert and Cold-War theoretician, George Kennan, one of the most prominent US diplomats, became the Ambassador in that historical year, 1961, and remained until 1963.

In mid-March 1963, he was succeeded by Charles B. Elbrick, the Ambassador who spent six years in Belgrade. He witnessed the re-tightening of the relations between Belgrade and Moscow in 1968, after the events in Czechoslovakia, and the first greater internal riots in Yugoslavia, when students' demonstrations broke out in Belgrade and students' riots in Pristina, which were hidden from the Serbian public. At the time, one of the officials in the Embassy was Warren Zimmermann.

When Elbrick left in June 1969, Ambassador William Leonhart took of ice and he had one primary task – to prepare the first official visit of the US President to Yugoslavia. Richard Nixon stepped onto the Yugoslav soil in 1970. Returning home to Washington, he took Ambassador Leonhart with him. Instead of him, at the end of October 1971, Malcom Toon came to Belgrade. He was a quite calm and serious diplomat, which cannot be said for his successor Laurence Silberman.

The moment he took the of ice, in 1975, Silberman started publicly criticizing Yugoslav self-government and violation of human rights, as well as the failure to comply with the Helsinki Convention. In the official Yugoslav circles it was interpreted as the CIA action to bring instability in Yugoslavia, so Josip Broz publicly accused the US Ambassador for the anti-Yugoslav action. Although Ambassador Laurence Silberman had great merits in the arrival of the second US president to Yugoslavia in 1975, when Gerald Ford visited Belgrade, Silberman was declared undesirable, so the official Washington withdrew him from Belgrade in the summer of 1977.

Ambassador Laurence Silberman

The USA then sent Lawrence Eagleburger, who had the task to build diplomatic relations with Yugoslavia. The new Ambassador put such an effort in that, at one point, he even became a mediator in the Yugoslav economic affairs on the US soil. It is said that Eagleburger was an advocate for the placement of the Yugo Florida cars in the USA. He was also a connoisseur of the political situation in Belgrade, Zagreb, and Ljubljana, and he sent the information on the illness of Josip Broz Tito and his potential successor to the USA.

At the beginning of 1992, President Borisav Jovic talked with Lawrence Eagleburger, the former US Ambassador and Secretary of State, in Washington. Then, Eagleburger diplomatically deceived Jovic and Yugoslav public, because he declared that the USA wouldn't support the secession of Slovenia and Croatia and emphasized that the USA would in no way directly engage in the resolution of the Yugoslav crisis.

The US Ambassador Lawrence Eagleburger

The US media reacted to that statement with a cartoon depicting Lawrence Eagleburger as a bribed politician working for Serbs because they had paid him to represent the *Yugo America Project.*

Eagleburger, later, took back a part of his statement and said to Bora Jovic that he didn't know the definite attitude of the USA in relation to the recognition of individual Yugoslav republics. When the Serbian

Prime Minister Zoran Đinđic was murdered on 12th March 2003, Ambassador Lawrence Eagleburger came to his funeral.

MY FRIEND SCANLAN

After the death of Tito, in September 1980, the new US Ambassador in Yugoslavia was David Anderson. Several days after him, the third American President, Jimmy Carter, came to visit Belgrade. David Anderson was the Ambassador for five years and he witnessed the first disintegrative processes in the SFRY. That ambassadorial experience from Yugoslavia helped him later, upon his return to the USA, to become the greatest expert for the Balkans and the SFRY at the Aspen Institute in Berlin.

In 1985, Anderson was replaced by John Scanlan, a former diplomat from the US Embassy in Belgrade. He knew Serbian language very well and he was open for cooperation with Yugoslav politicians and businessmen. The Ambassador John Scanlan was honest and open towards me. The former US Ambassador John Scanlan got acquainted with Milosevic at the time when he was the deputy of Lawrence Eagleburger:

"We met when Slobodan Milosevic was the President of Beobanka. At the time, we, the Americans, didn't see him as a political leader, but just as a quite young bank president. We didn't anticipate that he would become the future leader of Yugoslavia, and we didn't consider anyone powerful enough to be able to lead Yugoslavia after Tito's death. Milosevic was a banker, a friendly and intelligent man. He spoke English well and understood international banking a lot. I started seriously thinking about Milosevic as the leader of this country in 1986 or 1987. Not before that. I was even quite surprised when I came back in 1985 and saw that he wasn't in banking anymore. He was the Head of the City Committee, while the Head of the Party was Ivan Stambolic. At the time, there was a list of people we had a good relation with and, among them, Milosevic was one of the last ones. We didn't see Milosevic as a potential leader until 1987. Then he started breaking through," said Scanlan.

The US Ambassador John Douglas Scanlan

Milosevic's break-through on the political scene of the SFRY and Serbia was a topic of the reports that Ambassador Scanlan and the Secretaries of the US Embassy in Belgrade wrote and sent to Washington. The Ambassador openly spoke to me about that:

"We reported to Washington on Serbian rallies and on Milosevic having the support of 95% of Serbian people. He tried to decrease the autonomy of the two provinces in Serbia, so, at the beginning, Serbian people had a tangible right to complain and protest, until it all became too militant, too emotional, with the rise in warfare nationalism."

I, Borko Djordjevic, a Serbian citizen, leaving Yugoslavia, left behind a happy people and country. I returned in 1986, when the chaos started in the SFRY. The republic governments were in strife, the Albanian lobby was attacking Serbia, and Slovenian and Croatian politicians joined that attack. As an American citizen and a Serb, I told this to the then US Ambassador John Scanlan in the US Embassy in Belgrade. He responded in words that froze my blood:

"The USA has no interest in the SFRY. After Tito, this country is insignificant to the USA. There's nothing to be done here."

Ambassador Scanlan was absolutely right then, in 1986. Until 1980, Tito worked for the USA. He was a friend of Jimmy Carter and he negotiated with the Soviets on his behalf. Josip Broz was persuading Leonid Brezhnev, the President of the USSR to sign the treaty with the USA on the restriction of nuclear weapons. When Tito died in 1980, the new presidents of the SFRY didn't know how to work either with the Americans or with the Soviets. Yugoslavia was rapidly losing its international reputation and becoming an irrelevant country in the Balkans.

The Prime Minister Ante Markovic, facing a strong resistance of the Communists, didn't succeed in implementing reforms and introducing capitalism in the system of Yugoslav self-government. His greatest contribution was the establishment of free world market in the SFRY and the opening of credit facilities for the citizens of Yugoslavia.

I was personally concerned about the events that were fraught with nationalistic charge, which made nations fight to that extent that I realized it was a political war among Belgrade, Zagreb, Ljubljana, and Pristina.

In September 1987, I sent an appeal to John McCain, a Senator and a member of Reagan's political elite:

"Save Yugoslavia! It's time the USA came to the SFRY and helped it!" An old Communist spoke through me, wishing good to Yugoslavia and the Serbian people that lived united and in one place in this country. An American also spoke through me, believing that if the USA had held Tito's Yugoslavia and made it into a bridge to the USSR and the world leader of the non-aligned countries, my homeland, without Broz, could remain under the influence of the USA and quickly conduct its "perestroika".

In that letter to Senator John McCain, who was the head of the Republican Presidential Task Force since 1987, I sought advice in relation to the foreign politics towards the SFRY.

"There are some dramatic changes taking place in Yugoslavia which ought to be of concern to the USA. I had a long talk with Ambassador Scanlan and he agrees with me. Because of poor economic conditions, Yugoslavia is on the verge of a Civil War. I think that most of the leaders of the present Yugoslav Government recognize that, in talking to them I believe they are ready to accept 'the American way' if properly approached. I still believe that America still has a vital interest in this part of the world, considering how much was invested in Yugoslavia. I think this is the time to collect. Please advise how we are to go about it," I wrote to the American Senator John McCain.

Yugoslavia was the country with hard-working and good people. With American economic aid and loans, the life was good. That money was the key to the rule of Josip Broz Tito. At each session of the Central Committee of the League of Communists of Yugoslavia, the most important item on the agenda was a discussion on the economic situation and foreign exchange in low from abroad, where great Yugoslav companies operated. Yugoslavia earned billions of dollars abroad and provided social peace in the country. Milosevic tried to preserve that by destroying the SFRY and making the new, third Yugoslavia, as the country of all Serbs and the heaven for party elite and the Milosevic family.

Borko B. Djordjevic, M.D., Inc.
PLASTIC AND RECONSTRUCTIVE SURGERY

BEVERLY HILLS MEDICAL TOWER
1125 S. BEVERLY DR., SUITE 720
LOS ANGELES, CA 90035, U.S.A.
TEL: (213) 556-6404

COSMETIC SURGERY CENTER
1391 N. PALM CANYON DR.
PALM SPRINGS, CA 90262, U.S.A.
TEL: (619) 320-9702

September 14, 1987

Senator John McCain
Chairman Republican Presidential Task Force

Dear Senator McCain:

As a charter member of the Republican Presidential Task Force I'am writing this letter in order to seek your advice, which relates to foreign policy in relation to Yugoslavia.

Being a native Yugoslavian and citizen of the USA and vitaly interested in events taking place in Yugoslavia over the last year and a half, I've been to Yugoslavia four times, as a private citizen as well as a businessman.

There are some dramatic changes taking place in Yugoslavia which ought to be of concern to the USA. I had a long talk with Ambassador Scanlon he agrees with me. Because of poor economic conditions Yugoslavia is on the verge of a Civil War. I think that most of the leaders of the present Yugoslavian goverment recognize that, in talking to them I believe they are ready to accept "The American Way", if properly approached. I still believe that America still has vital interest in this part of the world and considering how much was invested in Yugoslavia, I think this is the time to collect.

Please advise how we go about it.

Sincerely,

Borko Djordjevic, M.D.

The letter of Dr Borko Djordjevic, MD, sent to Senator John McCain depicting the civil war and the disintegration of the SFRY and inviting the USA to pay attention

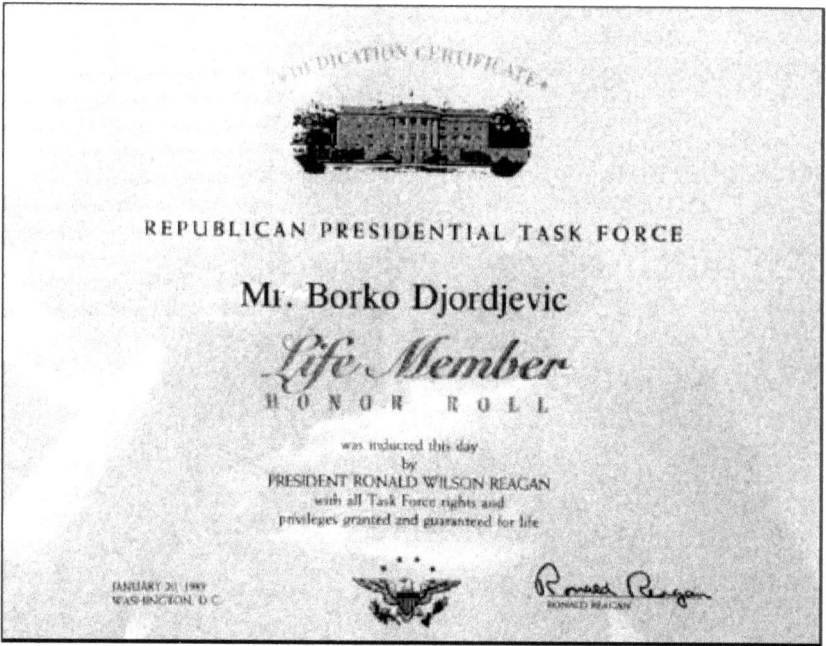

The Certificate of the Republican Party and the President Ronald Reagan to the Dr Borko Djordjevic, 1989

ZIMMERMAN'S FIRM

Tito's Yugoslavia was actually a multinational company with high foreign exchange income and pro it. That is why it was quite attractive to the American business and comfortable life. The USA was paying back Yugoslav foreign exchange debts in dollars and they were, investing in Serbia through its ambassadors and businessmen. Scanlan was arranging the entry of *Galenika* into the American pharmaceutical industry and he was one of the advisors of Milan Panic, the owner of *Galenika Inc.*

And, coming back home, I was trying to be an American and a businessman, but at the same time I wanted to be a Serb and a patriot. In Vienna and Geneva, in 1989, I opened a foreign trade company Atalanta, through which I supplied duty-free shops around Yugoslavia. I did that job with *Srbijaturist* company and its Director Đukic.

In Lausanne, I met Armin Aeberhard, a representative of *Philip Morris* company for the Balkans and got him married to a Serbian woman. To express his gratitude, he appointed me the exclusive representative of *Philip Morris* company for Yugoslavia. In that capacity, I reached an agreement between *Philip Morris* and *Nis Tobacco Industry* on the privatization of this factory of ours, which would, after modernization, produce as many as 12 billion cigarettes per year. The agreement was signed by my friend Armin Aeberhard.

Working for *Philip Morris*, I met, in Switzerland, our businessman Mirko Vucurovic and Ambassador Nebojsa Dimitrijevic, who was the representative of the SFRY in the UN Mission in Geneva. Americans valued him as an expert for biological weapons and Slobodan Milosevic hated him because he was a friend of Zoran Đinđic. Thus, he removed him from that post. I realized, then, that the spirit of Tito's system had died in the SFRY and that a new Serbian archon had come to power and he didn't care for old Yugoslavia and its excellent professionals.

The Prime Minister Ante Markovic submitted all the data on the economic power of the SFRY to the IMF and the USA stating that Yugoslav country had 10 billion dollars in cash in its treasury and the economy worth more than 100 billion dollars.

At the time, I had a clinic in Igalo and I used hotels when I came to Belgrade. I was having a dilemma on what to do. I couldn't stay in Montenegro any longer, because a conflict with Albanians, Slovenians, and Croats had started in Serbia. My Serbia needed me. I closed my surgery in Igalo and moved to Belgrade in 1990. I rented a space in *Genex Apartments* in New Belgrade. Little did I know that by moving to *Genex Apartments*, I entered the political nest of socialists, their political elite, police, and tycoons. In this green glass building on the Sava River quay, they had their operative headquarters.

The moment I came back to Belgrade, in 1990, I renewed my acquaintance with Vlada Stambuk, and Slobodan Braca Prohaska, who had become the Vice-President of the Government of Serbia. They accepted me as one of their own and as a sympathizer of the SPS. I participated in the elections in December 1990 on the side of Slobodan Milosevic, against Dragoljub Micunovic, as the presidential candidate.

After the victory of the SPS in 1991, Braca Prohaska introduced me to the Prime Minister Dragutin Zelenovic and the future Prime Minister Dr Radoman Bozovic. That is how I, completely unexpectedly, entered Serbian politics and business.

I also established by company *Atalanta* in Belgrade in 1991, when I tried to realize the business of introducing the system of purchasing by leasing. In that manner, 200 buses and cars were supposed to be procured for the Yugoslavian market, but that business failed. A year later, I established a company *Mak Moris* in Skopje.

However, I continued to give warnings that the SFRY would collapse and that it could take us, the people from Serbia, down the abyss with it. For almost five decades, Josip Broz and his communists were building their self-governing empire, which was facing its collapse at the beginning of '90s because of a political conflict within the country and the unsuccessful transition. I said all that to the Americans, but also to my comrades and friends in Belgrade. All of them considered Dr Borko Djordjevic just a ditz from the USA, a know-all who is unable to do anything.

In 1996, the Ambassador John Scanlan visited Belgrade again, now as the Director of the American Business Council for the FRY. Apart from his other functions, he was also a high consultant of the *ICN* company in California, managed by Milan Panic. This was the first meeting of the American Business Council for the FRY because the meetings couldn't be held during the UN sanctions.

The host of the gathering in Belgrade was the Yugoslav Chamber of Commerce. This was an opportunity for Ambassador Scanlan to renew old business connections and I was trying to do the same – to renew the old and establish the new connections and affairs.

The US Ambassador Warren Zimmermann

John Scanlan spoke Serbian and that is the reason he was a welcome guest in Belgrade. The new Ambassador Warren Zimmermann also spoke Serbian, but he seemed to be less friendly inclined towards Belgrade and the Serbs than his predecessor. I didn't have much contact with him. He came to the position of the Ambassador in 1989 from the American delegation in CSCE. Zimmermann willingly left Belgrade in 1992, after which the USA sent just a Charge d'Affaires William Montgomery.

After leaving Yugoslavia in 1992, Zimmermann was engaged as the Director of the Global Refugee Program in the US Government, but two years later, he left diplomacy and returned to being a professor and journalist. He wrote a book of memories *Yugoslavia and its Destroyers – Origins of a Catastrophe*, in which he confessed that he'd been making reports for the CIA:

"At the end of 1990, we had no more illusions. We knew that Yugoslavia, unless it survived, would disappear in a bloodbath," Warren Zimmermann wrote.

The American Ambassador Warren Zimmermann never had a nice opinion on Slobodan Milosevic, or on Serbia, which he treated as his failed firm. The reason for that may have been the fact that they were in constant conflict, since Zimmermann could not refrain from interfering into the internal affairs of the Republic of Serbia. Zimmermann and Milosevic weren't on speaking terms for a long time because of Kosmet. The President of Serbia was also angry because the Ambassador didn't appear in Gazimestan in 1989 at the celebration of six centuries since the Kosovo Battle. By his non-attendance, Zimmermann caused the absence of several more important diplomatic representatives of foreign countries in Belgrade. Zimmermann justified his non-attendance by an offensive statement that he disapproves nationalistic fairs and celebrations, even if they were the celebration of a great historical battle, crucial for the Serbian people in the Balkans.

In his memoires, referring to contacts with Lawrence Eagleburger, the US Ambassador Warren Zimmermann wrote about the Serbian President the following:

"Eagleburger confessed he was having some reserves in relation to the renewal of his acquaintance with Milosevic, who he'd met in the late 1970s, when he was the US Ambassador to Yugoslavia, and Milosevic was a banker. 'I thought he was a liberal; he talked so convincingly about westernizing Yugoslavia's economy. I just must have been wrong.'"

I don't think Eagleburger was wrong. Upon his return to Yugoslavia, Eagleburger could see the brand-new skin color of the most sophisticated chameleon in the Balkans. Eagleburger expressed his concern over the fact that Yugoslavia was rushing into nationalism, separatism, and major violations of human rights.

"Why are you blaming Serbia for this? Are you saying that we're the only ones responsible?" asked Milosevic.

"My impression is that all of you are responsible," the former Ambassador Eagleburger countered.

Milosevic rejected Eagleburger's insisting on human rights. The Assistant Minister replied:

"The USA has a legitimate obligation to defend human rights. In addition to that, we have the right to decide how we're going to spend the money of our tax payers or advise our business people in which countries to invest their capital. The decision on whether to give the priority to the countries with good state of human rights is made exclusively by us and nobody else," Warren Zimmermann wrote.

When political issues are concerned, Milosevic claimed that unified Yugoslavia was the only political formation which could make it possible for all the Serbs to live in one country. His formula for unity was uncompromising – a tight federation with minimal autonomy for the republics, claimed Ambassador Zimmerman.

At the beginning of his rule, Milosevic professed not to have anything against a multiparty system, but stressed it had to operate on a Yugoslav and not a republic basis:

"That wouldn't work," he stated.

It turned out he represented the preservation of Yugoslavia, but in a rigid manner that pandered the Serbian interests the way Milosevic perceived them. He said something that would soon take an ominous tone:

"Serbs live all around Yugoslavia. Only united Yugoslavia makes it possible for them to live in one country."

Dear Dr. Djordjevic:

Thank you for your support of the NRSC, and for all you do for our Party and its principles. This is so important to passing our compassionate conservative agenda and moving our nation forward.

US President George W. Bush expresses his gratitude for the support of Dr. Djordjevic

FROM BUSH TO CLINTON

When, at the end of 1980s and the beginning of 1990s, the USA faced the disintegration of the SFRY, they irst formulated their attitude as a crisis on the European soil, which should be solved by the Old Continent, and then as a democratic process. That marked a new period of strong US action towards Serbs. The US interest was to enable democratization, i.e. to prevent the action of the YNA, an instrument of the communist rule, and to support the republics that seceded from the SFRY.

According to the estimation of General Veljko Kadijevic, the USA and Europe wished to destroy the communist socialism in the SFRY in two ways first, immediately, with demonstrations, as in Poland and Hungary, with the risk of breaking up the country of Yugoslavia, as well, and secondly, with a slower penetration of anti-socialistic, pro-American, and capitalist ideology into the country.

At the end of 1989, Dr Borisav Jovic witnessed in his memoires that the YNA estimated that the West, more precisely the USA, would opt for the second version of destroying the Yugoslav communism. The reason for that was the fear of the Russians and their support to Serbia, because Moscow wanted to retain "their" Montenegrin access to the Adriatic Sea.

The aggression of the USA against Yugoslavia always depended on the aggression of the White House foreign politics. At the time of the beginning of Milosevic's rule and Yugoslav war drama, the President of the USA was a Republican Ronal Reagan, from 1981 to 1989. I was Reagan's Commissioner for California. Reagan believed that Milosevic, the same as Gorbachev, was a Communist that wanted democracy and reforms in his country. He supported Slobodan Milosevic and his reformed communist party – the Socialist Party of Serbia (SPS).

The following term of office in the US elections went to another Republican, George Bush Senior, who ruled from 1989 to 1993. As an experienced CIA Director and a cunning president, he knew about me and my secret yearning. He knew that Borko Djordjevic from Palm Springs cherished muffled love towards his homeland, Serbia. Bush himself told me that and I wasn't surprised. I wasn't even angry at Bush Senior because what he said was my truth. He knew I was loyal to the Republican Party and the USA and he didn't treat me as an object of his spy nature. He appreciated I was constantly thinking about my homeland and the people in it.

At the time of my first decade in the USA, while I was studying, working, and partying, I was also incessantly planning, but always postponing my trip to Serbia. It was easier to bring my dearest and closest to the USA than to constantly rush to Belgrade to see them. I brought my father and mother, and then sisters and brothers-in-law to California. My father Branko, who spent seven years in the USA, liked to feel important and to say to the Americans:

"I'm the father of Dr Djordjevic."

Bush Senior, as the President, offered Milosevic, through his envoys, to perform the transition of Serbia and Yugoslavia, to make our country the first in the region of Eastern Europe that would introduce private property and the capitalist system with the free market and foreign capital low. It was believed in the USA that Milosevic, as a politician, but also as a banker, was so rational that he could comprehend that transition was leading him directly into history books as a reformer and ensuring him a long rule. Milosevic accepted that proposal of Washington, but then he rejected it with a silent boycott and, thus, deceived George Bush and the Americans. Apart from Milosevic, the USA punished the FRY and Serbian people by imposing international sanctions that destroyed the economy, society, and morale of the Serbian people.

The US President George H. W. Bush, the official portrait in 1989

The Democrat Bill Clinton defeated Bush Sr. and was the US President for two terms, from 1993 to 2001. Clinton first made Milosevic into the "Butcher of the Balkans" and, then, into a peacemaker. He accused him of everything evil committed in the former SFRY and imposed Radovan Karadzic as his rival and the new Serbian archon. Then, he again placed his trust into

Milosevic, as the ruler of all the Serbs, to make peace with the Croats and the Muslims. Actually, Clinton estimated well that he would benefit more from Milosevic than from Karadzic and that Milosevic would make all American wishes come true.

As much as George Bush Sr., the former CIA Director, was inconsistent and indecisive in his attitude towards the SFRY, in respect to its preservation, that much was Bill Clinton, a sworn opponent of the CIA, in favor of the direct warmongering involvement into the resolution of the crises in former Yugoslavia. The first thing Clinton did, in 1994, was to obtain the open support of Europe and Russia for interventionism in the Balkans, and then to form a negotiating team of Richard Holbrooke, who brought all the three warring sides, Serbs, Croats, and Bosnians, to sign the Dayton Agreement in December 1995.

The war in Yugoslavia started as the clash of big powers over their political spheres of influence in the Balkans. For Americans, the penetration into the Balkans represented the entry into the European, and particularly Moscow influence zone. The Americans entered the Balkans quite easily in 1993 and 1994, so in 1996 and 1997, they didn't want to leave it, especially, as there was the rise in the political conviction of Bill Clinton, Hilary Clinton, and the military leadership in Washington that the USA were the only world rulers at the end of 1990s.

The US President William Bill Clinton, from 1993 to 2001

Ronald Reagan and George Bush imposed the role of the USA as the world ruler and police officer. At the end of 1980s, the two of them revived the spirit of the Cold War in the international relations. The Presidents Reagan and Bush taught the Americans to hate Europe and Europeans because they couldn't realize why the Old Continent wasn't following them in their offensive politics of the creation of the new world order.

For Bill Clinton, the US entry to the Balkans, more precisely to former Yugoslavia, was another diplomatic and political point before the new Presidential elections in the USA and, then, the reflection of the real power of the USA to rule the world. Bill Clinton then ordered the bombardment of Serbia and Montenegro, and defeated Slobodan Milosevic and Serbia.

Yugoslavia directly felt the power of the USA for the first time in mid-November 1990, when the US Ambassador Warren Zimmermann, the representative of the USA in the SFRY, warned Budimir Loncar, the Minister of Foreign Affairs that the CIA had made an analysis with a firm stand that the disintegration of Yugoslavia would occur and that its preservation would be attempted by a military coup. This was actually a message to the SFRY Presidency that the USA knew what was going on in Belgrade, accompanied by the false restraint of Zimmerman which he expressed by stating that he and the State Department didn't agree with the CIA assessment.

On the Republic Day in 1990, Zimmerman asked Bora Jovic whether the YNA would intervene in Slovenia if it attempted to secede. When the President of the SFRY Presidency replied negatively, Zimmerman sent his report to the White House the same night. At the same time, in the UN Security Council, the State Secretary Lawrence Eagleburger said to the Slovenes, on the behalf of the USA, that they could secede, because Americans were "more interested in the democratization than in the unity of Yugoslavia".

The American political leadership planned to execute that democratization process within the SFRY together with Slobodan Milosevic and the Government of Serbia, because Serbia was economically and politically the most powerful country in the Balkans at the beginning of 1990s. When the deal between Washington and Belgrade and the alliance between the USA and Milosevic failed, the Americans moved to political and military offensive.

NATO was the main political and military umbrella of the US initiatives for Yugoslavia and the USA had commanded it for more than twenty years. When the YNA started intervening in Slovenia in mid-1991, the west military alliance concluded that "Yugoslavia is one of key hotbeds of war in Europe and that is why the SFRY is the problem of the Old Continent and not just the Balkans". That is why it was decided to put a halt to any activity of the YNA, to have NATO prevent the flaring of the Yugoslavian crisis and to "take political and economic measures to mitigate that crisis". It was secretly decided in Washington not to return the American NATO military forces dislodged from Germany to the USA, but to send them to the Balkans.

However, in order to preserve his power, Slobodan Milosevic decided to activate the YNA, police forces, and Serbian paramilitary and parapolice formations in order to save post-Tito Yugoslavia. It would turn out that Milosevic did all that for himself, for his struggle for power over the Serbs, and for the political dream of his wife Dr Mira Markovic so that the two of them could be new Tito and Jovanka.

Washington then decided to illegally arm Muslim and Croatian army, through the CIA and DIA, and to train their officers and units to fight against the Yugoslav army of General Veljko Kadijevic, General Ratko Mladic, and Slobodan Milosevic, as the Supreme Commander.

WASHINGTON IN THE ANTECHAMBER OF WAR

"Yugoslavia will cease to function as a federal state within one year and will probably dissolve within two. Economic reform will not stave off the breakup," stated the report of October 1990 made by the American intelligence services, including CIA, for the government in Washington.

American spies estimated in 1990 that the Albanians in Kosovo would start "a long-standing armed uprising", but they failed to predict at the time the much more realistic conflict between the Serbs and the Croats. However, the administration of George Bush Sr. dismissed that intelligence estimate as overreacting and continued supporting the unity of the country. That wasn't the only great dissent between the government and intelligence regarding Yugoslavia and it was revealed in 2001 when most of the documents from the period from 1947 to 1990 were declassified.

The CIA conducted three analyses of the SFRY: the first in April, the second in October 1990, and the third at the beginning of 1991. The thirty-four original estimates, classified and confidential for a long time, were made public in 2001 for the conference named *From "National Communism" to National Collapse – Works of the US Intelligence Community Estimative Products on Yugoslavia 1948-1990.*

The secrets shared with the conference participants weighed five kilos. From the intelligence estimate NIE 15-90, created on 18th October 1990, I publish just segments that refer to the nine points of the future events in the SFRY:

The old Yugoslav federation is coming to an end, because the reservoir of political will holding Yugoslavia together is gone. Within a year, the federal system will no longer exist; within two years, Yugoslavia will probably have dissolved as a state.

Although elsewhere in Eastern Europe economic and political reform will be interdependent, Yugoslavia's future will be decided by political and ethnic factors. Even successful economic reforms will not hold the country together.

The forces within Serbia, Croatia, and Slovenia are a mix of national pride, local economic aspirations, and historically antagonistic religious and cultural identifications. In Slovenia, and to a lesser extent Croatia, the new nationalism is westward looking, democratic, and entrepreneurial.

In Serbia, it is rooted in statist economics, military tradition, and a preference for strong central government led by a dynamic personality.

Neither the Communist Party nor the Yugoslav National Army (JNA) will be able to hold the federation together. The party is in a shambles; the army has lost prestige because of its strong Communist Party identification and because much of the country considers it a Serb-dominated institution. No all-Yugoslav political movement has emerged to ill the void left by the collapse of the Titoist vision of a Yugoslav state, and none will.

Alternatives to dissolution now being discussed are unlikely to succeed. A loose confederation will appeal to Croatia and Slovenia, but Serbs will block this in an effort to preserve Serb influence. Moreover, a Serb-dominated attempt to muddle through will not be tolerated by the newly enfranchised, nationalistic electorates of the breakaway republics. Serbs know this.

It is likely that Serbian repression in Kosovo will result in an armed uprising by the majority Albanian population, supported by large Albanian minorities in Macedonia and Montenegro. This, in return, will create strong pressure on those republics to associate themselves closely with Serbia.

A slide from sporadic and spontaneous ethnic violence into organized inter-republic civil war is also a danger, but it is unlikely during the period of this Estimate. Serbia's commitment of resources to pacification of the Albanians in Kosovo will constrain its ability to use military means to bring Serbian minorities in the western part of the country under its direct control.

The Serbs, however, will attempt to foment uprisings by Serb minorities elsewhere – particularly in Croatia and Bosnia and Herzegovina and large-scale ethnic violence is likely.

The United States will have little capacity to preserve Yugoslav unity, notwithstanding the influence it has had there in the past. But, leaders from various republics will make claims on US officials to advance their partisan objectives. Federal and

Serb leaders will emphasize statements in support of territorial integrity. Slovenes, Croats, and Kosovars, however, will play up US pressure for improved performance on human rights and self-determination. Thus, Washington will continue to be drawn into the heated arena of interethnic conflict and will be expected to respond in some manner to the contrary claims of all parties.

The Soviet Union will have only an indirect influence – for example, through multinational forums – on the outcome in Yugoslavia. The Europeans have some leverage, but they are not going to use it to hold the old Yugoslavia together. Most of them, including the Germans, will pay lipservice to the idea of Yugoslav integrity, while quietly accepting the dissolution of the federal state.

All this, written in 1990, happened by the end of the 20th century. Americans knew the exact sequence of events because they were pulling all the strings. The saddest thing is that Slobodan Milosevic, intentionally or unintentionally, behaved in accordance with this political and war scenario.

David Binder, a former longtime *New York Times* correspondent from Belgrade, had an opportunity to see the 20-page-long analysis marked as *NIE 15-90* and its neutral title *Yugoslavia Transformed,* which bore many ominous predictions, such as the civil war and the deaths in the former SFRY.

"Because, six months later, in the intelligence estimate *NIE 15-90,* the CIA had different key conclusions, none of which offered any hope or promised the survival of the united Yugoslavia, as was the case in the previous estimate. In the *NIE 15-90* document, there was a page with the political map of Yugoslavia with marked borders of the republics and provinces. After it, there are Key Judgements summed up on two pages, and then the page representing the Contents of the report on 13 pages titled *Discussion.* That part starts with the quotation of a dialogue from a Wodehouse's book from 1928, in which a servant reports to his master that nothing had happened in the world that day, except some slight friction threatening in the Balkans," David Binder described this document.

Immediately, on the following page, there are the photos of two central actors – Josip Broz Tito and Slobodan Milosevic, and the third page is dominated by an illustration of London

Economist on which a huge Serb is sitting on a carriage on the representatives of all other smaller nations, while a decrepit and skinny cow is pulling such a carriage.

The entire page four is reserved for a text box on Kosovo, entitled *Kosovo – Yugoslavia's Killing Fields,* and the text box on the following page bears the title *Serbia's Difficult Choices.*

The entire page six and a half of page seven are devoted to Ante Markovic and his reforms. On page eight, there is a scheme and statistics on the economic gap between the North and the South of Yugoslavia, and the following page considers "an unlikely outcome".

The photos of the Slovenian and Croatian Presidents Milan Kucan and Franjo Tuđman are on page 10 and, after them, there is a map of the dissolution in Yugoslavia on which Slovenia and Croatia are separated from the rest of the country, Kosovo shaded with a dark, and Macedonia with a slightly lighter gray shade.

On page thirteen, there is the Annex with data on the ethnic composition of the republics and provinces, and on the next, the last page, there is a map of ethnic diversity in Yugoslavia."

The Key Judgements of the intelligence estimate NIE 15-90 represented a death certificate to the SFRY, an almost former country at the time. They left not even a trace of hope for the survival of Yugoslavia, and what was predicted was a hint of the upcoming catastrophe.

Gregory F. Treverton, the former Deputy Director of the National Intelligence Council (NIC), reviewing the intelligence operations during the '90s, starts his book of memoires with the following words:

"In the autumn of 1990, my predecessor in the National Intelligence Council predicted Yugoslavia's tragedy with a precision that is awe-inspiring. The National Intelligence Estimate concluded that Yugoslavia's breakup was inevitable. The breakup would be violent, and the conflict might expand... Yet, the estimate had no impact on policy whatsoever. None," honestly admitted Gregory F. Treverton.

After this document, the US Intelligence Community made a new NIE file on Milosevic, but not before 1994.

The CIA against Yugoslavia

POLITICAL COWBOYS

When it got involved in our drama, the USA changed its diplomatic perspective. The internal war of the SFRY became "Serbian aggression". Unheard-of sanctions were imposed on us and unprecedented media demonization was initiated. The USA became the chief arbiter in the political dissolving, splitting, and dividing of the second Yugoslavia.

At the beginning of 1995, Americans supported the Croatian operations *Storm* and *Flash* against the remains of the Serbian Krajina, creating the conditions for peace negotiations in Dayton. They bombarded us together with NATO in 1999, at the moment when President Bill Clinton was coming out of the difficult internal crisis after the scandal with Monica Lewinsky, in the circumstances when NATO had to finally be confirmed as a convincing alliance. With that, the USA verified its global leadership.

The US Embassy building in Kneza Milosa Street was first partially emptied in 1992. Before the beginning of the NATO bombing, in March 1999, practically everyone left the US Embassy. As the diplomatic relations of the third Yugoslavia (the FRY) and the USA were disrupted, American diplomats returned to the US Embassy only after the overthrowing of Milosevic, in 2000. The diplomatic relations of Washington and Belgrade on the ambassadorial level were restored on 17th November 2000, when William Montgomery, who had served in Zagreb, became the Ambassador in the FRY. He invested efforts in bringing Serbia and the USA closer.

In April 2001, President George Bush Junior met the Federal President Vojislav Kostunica and, in November, the Prime Minister Zoran Ðinđic. The highest US officials that came to Belgrade were the former Ambassador Lawrence Eagleburger, who also came to the Prime Minister's funeral, and the Secretary of State Colin Powell, who in April 2003 expressed his condolences to the family of the assassinated Zoran Ðinđic.

Ambassador Montgomery, known as Monty, was the US Ambassador in Belgrade from 15th November 2001 to February

2004. A Croatian journalist, Denis Kulis, called the diplomat William Montgomery "a green beret in the Balkan jungle".

Ambassador William Montgomery

He was born in 1946 in Carthage on the three-state border of Missouri, Kansas, and Oklahoma. As a diplomat, he served in Bulgaria for three years, until 1991, then in Budapest, and, after that, in Zagreb. He was a Special Envoy of the US President for Bosnian Peace Implementation. In Budapest, the Yugoslav Affairs Of ice was opened at the US Embassy.

Monty was the head of secret services of the USA on the region of the former Yugoslavia, the Security Advisor in the Government of Serbia, as well as a member of the Supervisory Board of the *Adriatic Luxury Hotels Group*. He had a strong influence in the calming of the situation in the south of Serbia in 2001, but also in the privatization of *Sartid* and the breakthrough of *Philip Morris* into the Serbian market. His influence on the government of Zoran Ðinđic and Zoran Zivkovic was apparent.

The Ambassador witnessed the extinguishing of Yugoslavia in its third edition in 2003. William Montgomery publicly fought for the survival of this new country, the State Union of Serbia and Montenegro, created in 2003, while, diplomatically, he continuously worked on preventing that from happening. The Union disintegrated in 2006 with Montenegro seceding from it.

Since then, the independent country of Serbia has existed. In that new country, Ambassador Montgomery became a businessman, doing business even with state public companies.

His successor, a not so widely known diplomat, Michael Polt, as the US Ambassador continued working on the political promotion of the USA in the, now, democratic Serbia. In a discussion with the Serbian Minister of Finance, Mlađan Dinkic, Polt amicably said that the USA was ready to maximally assist the Government of Serbia on one condition –that the first man of finances did not get involved in the military reform.

The following day, Dinkic attacked the Fund for Military Reform claiming it wanted to sell out the military property. Mr. Polt was astonished. That is how the affair "Military-Technical Institute", which the USA wanted to buy as the new Embassy, got opened. Dinkic prevented that and Serbia gave to the USA Tito's Of ice of the Marshal in Dedinje, where the construction of the building of the new US Embassy was started.

If Michael Polt resembled a cowboy, his successor Cameron Munter was a jazz-loving pianist. Munter was appointed the Ambassador in Serbia on 26th July 2007, after the USA had recalled Michael Polt because they were, as most people in Serbia, dissatisfied with his work. In Belgrade, at the beginning of 2007, he spoke that the Americans had no interest in punishing Serbia and causing any troubles here. However, during the ambassadorial term of Cameron Munter, the USA caused and supported unanimous proclamation of the Kosovo independence, for which the official Serbia mostly blames the USA.

Munter experienced the Serbian burning of the US Embassy. At the same time, he was the first US Ambassador to lay a wreath to Serbian victims of the NATO bombing. He advocated for the European Serbia. He behaved in a professional manner, as a diplomat, and not as a politician, which is very important in American-Serbian relations. Before leaving Belgrade, he organized the visit of the Vice President of the United States, Joseph Biden, to Serbia. After that, the Ambassador Cameron Munter stated:

"American-Serbian relations are multidimensional and successful."

By that, he left a legacy to Belgrade and Washington and particularly to the new US Ambassador.

Barack Obama, the new US President, appointed Mary Warlick the Ambassador in Serbia on 23rd September 2009. The arrival of Ambassador Mary Warlick marked the beginning of the works on the new US Embassy building, but also on the new CIA center in Belgrade. It was said that high US officials would come to the opening of the new US Embassy building in Serbia, maybe even the President Barack Obama.

The Ambassador Warlick was said to be a professional diplomat, an economic expert, and an expert for Russia. A professor of political sciences at the time, Predrag Simic, told me that Mary Warlick was a good choice for Serbia. Her first task was to regain the Serbian trust into the USA, i.e. to show the good will for cooperation and assistance to the official Belgrade in the process of the democratization of the country, and to influence the promotion of Serbian-American relations. It turned out that Ambassador Mary Warlick was just a diplomatic clerk, the same as the new Ambassador Michael Kirby, who was appointed in 2012. Kirby stood out in the Serbian public with his statement that "Serbia doesn't need Russia". By that, the USA announced the beginning of their political campaign against the influence of the official Moscow to Belgrade and against the strengthening of the relations between Serbia and Russia.

When Ambassador Kirby left Belgrade, he was succeeded by a Croatian and Zagreb son-in-law, Ambassador Kyle Scott, who speaks Serbian well, but who has continued accusing Serbia for its ties to Russia in a much more aggressive manner. He even stated that the Russian humanitarian center in Nis is actually a "Russian military base".

Scott served in Bulgaria, Montenegro, and Croatia, so he had acquired a great diplomatic experience in the Balkans. He behaved as a political cowboy. He tried disciplining Serbia and criticizing the President Aleksandar Vucic. However, with the arrival of Donald Trump to power, Ambassador Scott started changing his diplomatic rhetoric and the aggressive critical tone of his remarks. He marked the hundred years of the alliance victory of Serbs and Americans in the Great War by raising Serbian lag on the building of his residence. He made a television video on the Serbs as "great people" and promised to raise the Serbian lag on the roof of the White House in fall 2018, as happened in 1918 by the orders of the then President Woodrow Wilson who respected the Serbian people.

The US Ambassador Kyle Scott

During 136 years of the diplomatic and political relations between the USA and Serbia, there were officially around thirty American envoys and ambassadors in Belgrade. They operated as an extended arm of the US administration, reflected in the US President, State Department, Congress, and the US Senate. Their role was quite politically active, considering the fact that, as many believe, the USA is the key factor of the distribution of influence zones of the great powers in the Balkans.

It shouldn't be forgotten that we were bombarded two times by the US military forces, in 1945 and in 1999. The first time it was at the request of Josip Broz Tito and the second time because of the political stubbornness of Slobodan Milosevic towards the international community. It shouldn't be forgotten either that some diplomats, like Wild West cowboys, were taking out their political verbal weapons and shooting at the Serbian Government and people in the middle of Serbia.

In the past years, the USA have directly performed their influence on Serbia by breaking up the SFRY, creating new countries from former Yugoslav republics, weakening Serbia by dissolving the union with Montenegro and taking away the Kosovo and Metohija Province. The United States did assist in the overthrowing of Slobodan Milosevic, both politically and financially, but they then weakened the rule of Vojislav Kostunica, Zoran Đinđic, and Boris Tadic, despite publicly proclaiming that they supported the democratic Serbia.

GREEN DOLLARS POLITICS

In the '90s, the United States used all the means, including even their secret services CIA, DIA, FBI, and NSA to put pressure on the Republic of Srpska, Montenegro, Serbia, and the FRY and force them to make concessions. Those pressures went as far as to directly threaten with making arrests on the Serbian territory of Dr Radovan Karadzic, General Ratko Mladic, Zeljko Raznatovic Arkan, and taking them to the Hague. According to the *Washington Post*, that plan was being considered for Slobodan Milosevic, as well.

All attacks of the USA and CIA on Serbia were conducted in the fifth phase of the degradation of our country under the motto of fight for democracy and against the dictatorship of a Communist, Slobodan Milosevic, and his wife Mirjana Markovic. In the mid-1990s, reputable magazines *Time* and *Newsweek* nicknamed the President of Serbia the "Butcher of the Balkans".

In 1998, before the war in Yugoslavia and during the ongoing offensive of Serbian police and the Yugoslav Army against Kosmet terrorists, the Americans even called Slobodan Milosevic the "Balkan Saddam Hussein". That wasn't strong enough to them, so in the middle of the NATO aggression, on 5th April 1999, while Shqiptars were fleeing from bombs abroad, a journalist Timothy Garton Ash named the President of Yugoslavia the "New Adolf Hitler". That claim was later publicly used by Jacques Klein, a US peacekeeper in Bosnia and Herzegovina.

All these sobriquets were used in order to demonize the Yugoslav President. That shows that the political conflict between Washington and Belgrade in the '90s was actually a private war of Slobodan Milosevic against the USA and Presidents George Bush and Bill Clinton. Milosevic entered that war without any allies, dragging the country of Serbia and the Serbian people with him as a shield. Behind that shield, Slobodan Milosevic attacked the United States, dared and contradicted them, knowing very well that the Washington cowboys' response would be harsh – political retribution and ire arms.

That private Milosevic's war against the USA became so serious that a public discussion was opened on Milosevic, Serbia, and Kosmet on 24th June 1998 in the Subcommittee on European Affairs in the US Senate.

"I can't imagine a person worse than the President of Yugoslavia," said Senator Alfonse D'Amato on Slobodan Milosevic at the time. This Republican Senator from New York then added:

"It's time the impunity of Milosevic ended. Mr. President, I've submitted a resolution to the Senate today stating that the United States consider there to be a reason to believe that Slobodan Milosevic, the President of the Federal Republic of Yugoslavia, has committed war crimes, crimes against humanity, and genocide and that the International Criminal Tribunal for former Yugoslavia ought to publicly indict him. He is definitely in the same rank as all Pol Pots in the world. Milosevic should be publicly labeled as a war criminal and this key step could help save lives. It would stop further ethnic cleansing and give wing to democracy," the Republican Senator Alfonse D'Amato proposed what most US politicians also believed.

And, the USA decided to bombard the country of Slobodan Milosevic and the people of the FRY through NATO. The pretext was found in the killings of the Albanians in Racak and the exodus of the Albanians from Kosmet to Macedonia, under the control of the state government. That movement had a "genocidal character" to the USA. It was a pretext for war of the West Military Alliance against Serbia.

In the evening of 24th March 1999, sirens announced the attack of *Merciful Angel*, as NATO code-named its murderous action against the FRY. Precisely 19 world countries, with their economic potential 600 times larger than the FRY at the time, justified the bombardment by stating it prevented humanitarian disaster in Kosovo and Metohija and destroyed the regime of Slobodan Milosevic.

During those 78 days, according to the estimations, up to 2,500 people were killed in the attacks. The Yugoslav Committee of the Red Cross announced that there were 79 children among the killed. Two-year-old Marko Simic and threeyear-old Milica Rakic were among the youngest ones killed in the attacks. They devastated the infrastructure, industrial facilities, schools, bridges, health institutions, media houses, cultural monuments, etc. Belgrade authorities estimated the damage at around 100 billion dollars and requested the compensation from the NATO members in a lawsuit.

The bombardment of the FRY was terminated on 10th June 1999 by adopting the Resolution 1244 of the UN Security Council. The day before that, the representatives of the Yugoslav Army and NATO signed the Military-Technical Agreement in Kumanovo. This Agreement envisaged the withdrawal of forces of the Yugoslav Army from Kosmet and the entry of international troops (KFOR) into the Province. That is how the Serbian province was turned into a US colonial state. After that, on 22nd November 1999, the US President Bill Clinton travelled to Kosmet to support the "Albanian victory" and promise Albanians their independence.

NATO bombarded Serbia because of Slobodan Milosevic

Ten years after the secession of Kosovo and Metohija, that Serbian Province is almost completely ethnically cleansed of Serbs. From 20%of Kosmet residents, Serbian people are now reduced to just 5% of its population.

However, it turned out that the war against the FRY didn't throw Slobodan Milosevic down and that the US strategy was unsuccessful. Milosevic presented the defeat in Kosmet as his and national sacrifice in the fight for freedom. He remained on power. One and a half months after the truce of 10th June 1999, the White House considered a new program for overthrowing Slobodan Milosevic and introducing the US democracy in Serbia. Instead of bombs, Americans decided to use the dollar.

On 30th July 1999, just before the Stability Pact Summit in Sarajevo, President Bill Clinton announced that his administration had allocated ten million dollars with the aim of introducing democracy in Serbia. This money would be provided from the available funds of the Support for East European Democracy (SEED). Entitled *Serbia Democratization Act 1999*, this draft contains a series of measures directed towards the rapid replacement of Milosevic:

- encouraging the Serbian opposition to create a common platform and develop a positive and progressive message;
- supporting the democratically elected government of President Djukanovic in Montenegro, including the finding of a suitable place for Montenegro within the Stability Pact;
- surrounding Serbia with a ring of transmitters of the radio stations *Voice of America* and the *Radio Free Europe* in order to oppose the propaganda of Milosevic's state media;
- continuing economic and other sanctions towards Serbia and refusing cooperation in the reconstruction of the country for as long as Slobodan Milosevic is on power;
- encouraging our allies and other countries that are participants in the Stability Pact to join these efforts.

Apart from these measures, in July 1999, the US Congress passed other punitive measures of the USA towards the third Yugoslavia: blocking entire Yugoslav property in the USA, prohibiting US loans or investments into Yugoslavia, prohibiting the exportation of computers and computer programs to the Governments of Serbia and Yugoslavia, prohibiting military cooperation of the USA and Serbian or Yugoslav military forces, prohibiting issuance of visas to the high officials of Serbian and Yugoslav government, but not to the Montenegrin officials. These measures included a remark the entire Congress agreed with:

President Bill Clinton is to encourage other countries to adopt similar measures.

Since Slobodan Milosevic didn't attend the Summit in Sarajevo, the United States sent an appeal to the people of Serbia and the FRY to accept the democratic changes:

"We are anxiously waiting for the day when the FRY will have the government that rejects the politics from the past decade and embraces democracy, human rights, rule of law, and international cooperation. Such government could lead Serbia into Europe and not the government that is led by an indicted war criminal."

Speaking on the final tactics of overthrowing Slobodan Milosevic, Robert Gelbard, the Special Representative of the USA said:

"I would divide the U.S. Government's efforts on Serbia democratization into five categories:

We are making sure that Milosevic remains completely isolated. This involves not just our sanctions policy and the visa ban, which has had a demonstrably negative effect on members of the Milosevic regime, but also The Hague Tribunal indictments.

We are beginning to assist a wide array of democratic groups, including NGOs, political parties, independent media, youth organizations, and independent labor unions.

We are consulting closely with European allies in order to coordinate our activities both on Kosovo and on Serbia democratization generally.

We are encouraging the active engagement of regional countries in southeast Europe to harness their expertise with democratization and transition.

We are providing strong support for the reform government in the FRY Republic Montenegro."

At his suggestion, the USA allocated 100 million dollars during a two-year period for the FRY democratization projects. To Montenegro only, the USA set aside 37 million dollars of aid and twenty million dollars to the Yugoslav independent media.

As Tim Marshall, a US journalist, explained in his book *Shadowplay*, the USA financed the people's putsch on 5th October 2000 with 65 million dollars in order to overthrow Slobodan Milosevic and Mira Markovic.

SANCTIONS, CRIME, AND MAFIA

And, while the USA and the international community were putting pressure on the FRY and Slobodan Milosevic from the outside, the archon was boiling inside in his own hot pot. Croatia and Slovenia had seceded and, in order to prevent the same thing from happening in Bosnia, Serbs started a war with the assistance of Belgrade.

The UN Security Council imposed sanctions on the FRY on 30th May 1992 accusing it to have participated in the civil war in Bosnia and Herzegovina. The Resolution 757 determined the complete international embargo of Yugoslavia. More precisely, Serbian companies from Serbia and Montenegro were forbidden to do foreign trade, to import raw material and goods, as well as to export their products and have foreign exchange transactions. The embargo was imposed on the production and sale of military and other weapons, which had been bringing significant pro it to the FRY.

Companies, whose workers, ever since 1986, had spent a great deal of time at the support rallies to Slobodan Milosevic and his party, now started losing work, workers, and money. There was a considerable lack of consumer goods, first of all the imported ones, such as coffee, cigarettes, alcohol, fuel, chemical products, even food. People started spending their foreign exchange savings, but that wasn't enough to get by.

Because of the embargo, black economy appeared, as well as illegal trade with stolen and smuggled goods of suspicious origin. Due to the lack of foreign exchange in low, the value of dinar decreased, and it was more and more frequently printed, which led to inflation. Banknotes of five billion dinars were printed and their value was just two days long.

Black economy was organized by state institutions, primarily by the Federal Customs Administration of the FRY and the State Security Service, which coordinated the illegal import and smuggling of fuel, cigarettes, foreign exchange, alcohol, food, weapons, cars, and narcotics. Serbian Secret Police and the Special Operations Unit (JSO), together with the Zemun drug cartel, sold to Serbian youths as much as sixty kilos of heroine per month.

This illegal black-market business was done by Serbian patriots and world mobsters. The nicknames of some of them are known to the public: Braca, Badza, Cane, Arkan, Legija, Duća... even Dr Mira Markovic is mentioned in the affair in relation to the smuggling of cigarettes which her son, Marko Milosevic, was suspected of. According to the writings of the *Blic*, pre-trial proceedings marked her as an important link in the business that brought millions to criminals.

Allegedly, it was the President's wife who gave the signal to the Head of Customs, Mihalj Kertes, which contingent of cigarettes to let by, that is, when to turn a blind eye so that her son Marko could swimmingly bring in cigarettes bought in Bulgaria and so that they could be miraculously transformed in the official record into furniture being dispatched to Hungary. The son avoided customs in that way and became the head of one of the most profitable business activities in the post-war Serbia. The money he earned during those years is estimated at several hundred million German marks.

Food was smuggled from Hungary, alcohol from the robbed beverage factories in Croatia, fuel from Bulgaria and Romania, cigarettes from Macedonia and Montenegro, foreign exchange from Greece, through which fake export business was being done, cooking oil from Switzerland... Some serious foreign businessmen of Serbian origin, such as Mr Mirko, for instance also participated in these activities.

Two men of the police, Arkan and Legija, who were the leaders of their (para)police forces in the fights against Albanian nationalists, terrorists, but also civilians, were building their mafia empires thanks to the black economy. The archon Slobodan Milosevic was familiar with both of them. Arkan established a political party and became a Member of the Serbian Parliament because he had done a good job in attracting the Serbian young into the membership of the SPS. And, Legija, who Sloba called by the pet name Cema, created drug mafia named Zemun Clan which became a state within a state.

Milorad Ulemek Legija and Zeljko Raznatovic Arkan

When Milosevic centralized Serbia, introduced police control and para-criminal groups, developed the activities of state smuggling and black market, the US Ambassador Warren Zimmermann reported to President George Bush on that. He wrote *The White Paper on Serbia* and sent it to the White House. Zimmermann, who was also well familiar with the Serbian language and the Serbian mentality, having worked as the Secretary of the US Embassy in Belgrade, described in that paper to the president George Bush all men surrounding Milosevic, from Sainovic to Zebic and Ckrebic, as "Little Slobas", cloned nationalists and arrogant politicians.

He reported that Arkan and Legija were persecuting Albanian civilians, who were robbed by Serbian para-soldiers and criminals, that Jezda and Dafina were fraudsters who, by offering fake high interests were actually taking foreign exchange from the hands of Serbian population. In order to simulate that Serbian economy was actually working, Milosevic was selling state companies for trifling sums to his businessmen. He printed money for their business ventures and they got rich and financed his country.

The international community knew about the black economy and smuggling, but it allowed Slobodan Milos-evic to acquire money, in this manner, which was necessary for the functioning of the party and the elite on power, but also of the country.

MY PERISHED MILLIONS

The fact is that the Americans still wished, secretly and despite the embargo, to revive the Serbian economy by indirect investments, through the privatization in Serbia.

During the sanctions, *Philip Morris Company* organized illegal tobacco trade around the world through its Rotterdam base, where it had the largest tobacco factory, and then in Russia, Macedonia, Italy, Switzerland, Montenegro, and Serbia. Cigarettes were re-packed, the bar code was changed, and they would travel around the world. They went from factories through Macedonia into Montenegro, Switzerland, and Italy. The cost of production was twenty-five cents per one cigarette pack and the sales price was as much as five dollars. Enormous pro it was generated, and it was used by the American lobby to finance the war in Yugoslavia.

If Milosevic had let *Philip Morris* privatize N*is Tobacco Industry,* this smuggling business wouldn't occur and, thereby, neither would the war in Yugoslavia. This cigarette smuggling business involved the Military Security Service, State Security Service, military company *Yugoimport SDPR*, military and civilian associates of the Secret Police, even reputable businessmen, doctors, and traders. The names mentioned were: Mirko Vucurevic, Lale Sekulic, Dr Ninoslav Radovanovic, and Stanko Subotic from Switzerland. Many people in Belgrade were making excellent pro its out of the war and cigarettes.

I was offered to be a cover for the illegal trade in cigarettes, travelling from Macedonia to Serbia and Montenegro and, then, in speedboats, further towards the Italian and European black market. I also had a company that traded with cigarettes until the point when the Zemun Clan mobsters, ordered by the Milosevic's men, seized ten containers of cigarettes from me. They were afraid I might get rich as well.

Due to the sanctions, inflation, and mafia in the third Yugoslavia, most of my business ventures failed. Because of the Yugoslav politicians and managers' wheeling and dealing, I didn't want to get compromised and involved in any criminal combinations. Whenever I had felt the breath of mafia and crime, I would have run away from that activity.

In order to rule smoothly, Milosevic needed a huge amount of money. People around him were instrumentalized to make money and take it from Serbia or to put it into their own pockets. For instance, the money he wrested from state companies, Milosevic transferred here and there, to Cyprus, to Russia, China, even Austria. He behaved like a firefighter and not a ruler. He put out the political ire and the lames of war, but he didn't build the system of protecting the people and country from disaster.

Slobodan Milosevic and Mirjana Markovic, as the masters of the country and Serbian people, feared that, through the process of privatization, they might lose state factories and state communist property that were the foundation of their political power. Milosevic was afraid that by losing money, he would lose the power.

THE WAR OVER BILLIONS

My conclusion is that Slobodan Milosevic, as the leader of Serbia and the head of the FRY, waged war not to save the country and the people, but to save Yugoslav billions for himself. He counted on the fact that he, as the ruler of the FRY, would inherit Yugoslav capital in foreign banks and the capital of foreign trade companies abroad.

Craving to obtain political power, but also personal wealth, Slobodan Milosevic and the members of his family organized taking foreign exchange out of the third Yugoslavia and their depositing on private accounts or accounts of offshore companies in Cyprus or other countries. According to the official records, fifteen billion dollars were taken out, and according to the unofficial information from the USA, around 47 billion marks were illegally taken out of the country.

Those activities included Borka Vucic, a banker from *Beogradska Bank*, Mihalj Kertes, the Director of the Federal Customs Administration of the FRY, and the directors of *JAT* airline company, which transported the foreign exchange. I watched bags of money going to Slobodan Milosevic and his family. *JAT* was transporting them to Cyprus into the *Cyprus Popular Bank.*

As one of the key persons that knew the path of the lost billions, Borka Vucic, the Director of *Beogradska Bank* in Cyprus during the sanctions, claimed on several occasions that there was no illegal transfer of the money abroad. Borka Vucic was considered the financial pillar of Milosevic's rule.

Slobodan Milosevic and Mira Markovic, the rulers of the FRY

In 1995, Borka called me to help her unblock four billion dollars of Yugoslav pro it that were lying in the US banks. It was the money earned from the export of weapons, cars, food, and Yugoslav films to the USA. She told me on several occasions that Slobodan Milosevic and Mirjana Markovic had 47 billion marks of state money at their disposal on different bank accounts. She estimated that it was risky to have that money in the state treasury and state banks, so she was planning to transfer it to Cyprus, and, from there, further to the Serbian-Russian bank that she would open in Moscow.

Mihalj Kertes was accused of taking around 38 million German marks to Cyprus from 1994 to 2000 without the approval of the *National Bank of Serbia* and that, following the orders of Slobodan Milosevic, he illegally paid more than 116 million marks of the customs money on the accounts of various natural and legal persons. For that, he was sentenced to six and a half years in prison, but that decision was cancelled by the Supreme Court of Cassation. At the beginning of 2014, Mihalj Kertes was acquitted of this charge because the case had become obsolete. At the same time, some persons charged with the organized smuggling and trade of cigarettes during the time of Milosevic were also acquitted.

Borka Vucic was assassinated in 2009 because she knew where the hidden money the Milosevic family had taken out of the country was. She was killed by Milosevic's successors in the DOS. I don't know whether she managed to open the bank in Russia for the needs of the Milosevic family and to remove the Serbian state money there, but I know that Dr Mirjana Markovic took shelter in Moscow and that can't be a coincidence.

There are some people in Serbia, from political parties, media, or just individuals, who claim that Mira Markovic took 5 billion dollars to Russia during her escape. Moreover, it is said that she created the discord between the FRY and Russia, which also voted for the Belgrade sanctions, because she didn't support President Boris Yeltsin, but his opponent, a Communist, Zyuganov.

Nowadays, political analysts and some media from Serbia speculate that Russian President Yeltsin was in the direct contact with Bill Clinton and that he supported him in the overthrowing of Slobodan Milosevic.

The fact is that Milosevic didn't have a vision how to get out of the war crisis and to conduct the transformation of Serbia into a democratic and capitalist state. Sloba was clear that he could only win the war and protect his family if he had enough money. When his wife, Mira Markovic realized that Slobodan Milosevic couldn't do that on his own, she established the JUL and asked from her party comrades, directors of Yugoslav and Serbian companies, to pay money to her. The capital they acquired in the FRY, Slobodan Milosevic and Mira Markovic stored in Vienna, Moscow, Singapore, Tokyo, and Cyprus. One Serbian tycoon used that money to buy the paintings of the greatest Serbian artists and to make a collection that is today worth at least one billion euros. It is said that Dr Mirjana Markovic, the wife of Slobodan Milosevic, used that state and people's money to buy diamonds in Japan, Singapore, and China, through her trusted people. A witness to that transaction of national money and diamonds could be Vlada Stambuk, who spoke to me about it, but he didn't want to testify publicly. As far as I know, today, Mirjana Markovic has a political asylum in Russia and lives from selling, slowly and individually, her diamonds from Japan, Singapore, and China.

The breakup of the SFRY started and happened because of money, because rich republics of Slovenia and Croatia didn't want to support poor regions, Macedonia, Bosnia, and Kosmet, any longer. Slovenia and Croatia wanted to conduct the transition, to remain wealthy, to become independent, and to lead their own politics. Also because of money, Slobodan Milosevic, as the president of Serbia, didn't want to renounce the state property of Yugoslavia and he started a war.

The Third World War in the Balkans, waged from 1992 to 1995 and, then, continued in 1999, proceeded according to the established historical scenario already seen in the Great War and the Second World War.

Yugoslavia, which Tito had been building for four decades, was disintegrated in five years. The YNA broke apart, and the Yugoslav economy collapsed. People were turned into beggars who had to run around every day in order to ind a job and make a living.

First, under the influence of Germany and Austria, the nationalists in Slovenia and Croatia sought independence, which was understood by the Serbian nationalists as the revival of fascism in the SFRY and the German ambition to establish the "Fourth Reich". The traditional Russian support to Serbs and Turkish support to Bosnian Muslims caused additional fears in other communities and spread the smell of war in the Balkans.

Despite the announcements of bloodshed in Yugoslavia, the international community didn't get involved in the conflict until the violence was well advanced. The US Secretary of State James Baker visited Belgrade in 1991, several days prior to the Slovenian and Croatian declaration of independence, and said that he hoped that Yugoslavia would remain united voluntarily and that the USA would not support unilateral declarations of independence and the use of force. Twelve ministers of Foreign Affairs of the European Community (EC) agreed that they didn't recognize unilateral declarations of independence.

The reality was that the international community didn't have a plan for resolving the situation that, at that point, had become inevitable. As the summer was turning into the fall and as the pictures of war between the YNA, dominated by Serbs, and Croatia became breaking news, the concern of the world community was increasing. In September 1991, the European Community appointed British Lord Peter Carrington a mediator in the conflict. At Carrington's objection, Germany started putting pressure on the international recognition of the two repatriated republics.

In December 1991, the UN appointed the former US Secretary of State Cyrus Vance its representative in peace negotiations. The Vance Plan, made at the end of December, envisaged the deployment of UN forces in three areas in Croatia under the control of Serbs in order to protect the people in them. In return, the YNA was supposed to retreat, to disband Serbian paramilitary forces, and to make a truce. In Croatia, Tuđman agreed with the Vance Plan, because Germany had convinced him that Croatia would be internationally recognized.

Milosevic, now effectively holding the YNA under control, agreed with it because that was his best opportunity to freeze the first front line and establish new de facto borders.

The UN Resolution 743 on February 1992 approved the deployment of the United Nation Protection Force (UNPROFOR). After the referendum boycotted by Bosnian Serbs, who were hoping to get international help in case of a war, Alija Izetbegovic got the independence of Bosnia and Herzegovina in March 1992. Leading politicians of the Bosnian Serbs declared their own Serbian Republic within Bosnia and Herzegovina, later named the Republic of Srpska. In the mid-1992, after Slovenia and Croatia had obtained their independence, the incomplete Federal Republic of Yugoslavia (FRY) was created.

Because of rejecting foreign partners, the Americans, and their 70 billion dollars for transition, i.e. accelerated democratization of the country, and because of causing war conflicts, the FRY lost three markets: in Europe, in Russia, and in the countries of the non-aligned in Africa and Asia. And, when there's no market, there's no production, no export, and no foreign exchange pro it.

MONEY AND POWER

Milosevic was neither a Serbian nor an American man. He was a Communist, a man without national faith and church. He was only interested in money and political power. He renounced the Serbs in Bosnia and Herzegovina and the Serbs in Croatia in order to more easily obtain the property of Yugoslavia and establish his power in the FRY. Defending his Communism, Milosevic destroyed Serbia, especially Kosmet and led all the Serbian people into misery.

He experienced the sanctions of the international community as a political war and not as an economic punishment. During the embargo, Milosevic shifted life from a public scene into the underground. The FRY secretly did business with Macedonia and Greece. Milosevic was a banker, but he knew nothing about the real business. He turned out to be a good organizer of the black economy, which experts named the gray economy because it had the protection of the country.

Milosevic didn't want to sell *Nis Tobacco Industry* to the Americans at its right cost in the beginning of the '90s, because, during the sanctions, he financed his political parties and the country with cigarette smuggling. During the sanctions, when his people were tremendously suffering, Milosevic was just fighting to obtain money and to remain on power. The Serbian archon obviously learned nothing from great Tito, for whom the people from Valjevo used to say that he had been the greatest Serbian Emperor.

Josip Broz democratized Yugoslavia by taking loans and business activities from the Americans and sharing the pro it with the people in his country. Tito gave the Americans the pro it and they gave him the world reputation. Slobodan Milosevic didn't want that or he didn't know how to do that. He took everything for himself, his family, his elite, and his mafia.

Back in 1992, Slobodan Milosevic promised the Americans that they could privatize the entire Yugoslavia and Serbia, but he got afraid that he would lose power by losing the capital, so he gave up the transition.

He deceived the Americans, who wanted to invest and earn billions of dollars in Serbia, and he deceived NATO, who is the guardian of the US capital. Milosevic didn't know that NATO's purpose in the USA and Europe is to protect the investments of multinational companies anywhere in the world. When Sloba rejected the investments of the new world order in the FRY and Serbia, worth 70 billion dollars, NATO bombarded us, the Serbs, for 78 days. He thought he could manage the country as a mafia company and the land of state tycoons. Slobodan Milosevic never realized that, by organizing the country as a machine for making personal capital, he was actually losing power and the country. With that, he was becoming powerless next to his wife and political partner, Mira Markovic, who was dragging him into violence.

Balasevic, the Director of *Duga*, a sympathizer of Mira, and Zoran Todorovic Kundak, a boyfriend of Mrs Markovic were especially responsible for making and protecting money. Kundak, with whom I travelled to Macedonia on business, told me that he wanted to leave Mira Markovic and JUL, because they were conducting political and family centralism. He had a lover and he was planning to have a family. It was later spoken around Belgrade that Mira Markovic had him killed because "Kundak betrayed her".

They had Vuk and Dana Draskovic, the people who seriously resisted them, beaten up. There were two assassination attempts at Vuk Draskovic. Vuk's associates were killed, as well as Dana's brother. Slavko Ćuruvija, a journalist and an opponent, was murdered. Ivica Stambolic, a political rival, was liquidated because he was planning to participate in the elections. Assassinations of Milo Djukanovic, a Montenegrin leader, were attempted. The executors were the members of the Serbian state police and state mafia. In that manner, with his political violence, Milosevic started destroying the FRY and Serbia from within. Together with his wife, he wished to have a complete political control over the FRY and parties.

Some reasonable finger-pointing was done at Mirjana Markovic, when the assassinations of Slavko Ćuruvija and Ivan Stambolic were concerned. According to the indictment, it was Mrs Markovic that organized the meeting with the leaders of the police and the State Security (DB) on which she arranged the details of the assassination of Ćuruvija on 11th April 1999. It was

142

also established that it was her that had ordered the publishing of the pamphlet "Ćuruvija welcomes bombs" in Politika Express and reading of it on RTS on 6th April, which actually placed a target on the head of the owner and editor of the daily newspaper Dnevni Telegraf and magazine Evropljanin, and labeled him as a traitor who hated his people and who would never be forgiven for that.

After the schism at the 8th Plenary Session and the final victory of Slobodan Milosevic, his former friend and colleague Ivan Stambolic vanished from the public scene. However, right before the elections in 2000, there was a serious rumor that Stambolic as the candidate of the united opposition would be the opponent of Milosevic. In the spring of that year, at the session of the JUL Directorate, Mirjana Markovic commented on the election strategy and stated: "We won't have a problem with the opposition. Our bigger problem will be the resurrected ghosts of the 8th Plenary Session."

As in the case of Ćuruvija, there was a short step from her word to the execution. It was the announcement of what was going to happen on 25th August that year, when Ivan Stambolic was kidnapped at the trim track in Kosutnjak and then brutally liquidated on Fruska Gora Mountain. His body was found during the operation *Sablja* (Saber) in 2003 and persons charged with his murder were: Branko Bercek, Milorad Ulemek, Dusko Maricic Gumar, Leonid Milivojevic, and Nenad Bujosevic, members of the Special Operations Unit (JSO), as well as Radomir Markovic, the former Head of the State Security (DB). The first two were sentenced to 40 years in prison each, which was the first sentence of that kind of the Special Court, and altogether to 205 years in prison.

The spouses Milosevic – Markovic were also suspected of causing the assassination of the Serbian Prime Minister Zoran Đinđic in the yard of the Government of Serbia on 13th March 2003, with the assistance of the Zemun Clan.

The opposition led by Zoran Đinđic had a support from Germany and it had received a task to overthrow Milosevic. With the assistance of the Americans and the Germans, Đinđic succeeded in that on 5th October 2000. Not long after that, he arrested Milosevic and in 2001, on the national and religious holiday, Vidovdan, unlawfully extradited him to the Hague War Crimes Tribunal, where Milosevic died.

By assassinating Đinđic, opposition claimed, Mirjana Markovic avenged her late husband.

Around a decade later, when Mira Markovic had already led abroad with her children and had been living nicely there, Sloba and Mira's policemen and criminals Rade Markovic and Milorad Ulemek Legija were sentenced to many years in prison for the assassination of the Serbian Prime Minister Zoran Đinđic.

Six wives of US Presidents

THE LIST OF DANGEROUS SERBS

The embargo to the country of Slobodan Milosevic was the real retribution for Serbian people because SPS and JUL persuaded their sympathizers and voters that, with their suffering and misery, they were resisting the Americanism and defending their poor freedom.

One of the measures of punishing the Serbs involved the "black lists" of the persons from our country that were forbidden to enter the USA. Those lists were made by Bill Clinton, George Bush Junior, and Barack Obama. All the three presidents of the USA were making these lists according to the data submitted by the CIA in Belgrade.

During the rule of President Bill Clinton, at the end of 1993, the USA, NATO, and the EU made and published the list of 600 undesirable persons that were forbidden from entering the West. The list included the members of the Milosevic family, the members of the FRY Government, the army members, SPS activists, and sympathizers of Slobodan Milosevic.

These people were forbidden to travel to the USA, because, in 1993, they became undesirable and dangerous Serbs: Slobodan Milosevic, the President of the FRY, his wife Mirjana Markovic, his brother Borislav Milosevic, his daughter Marija Milosevic, his son Marko Milosevic, and his daughter-in-law Milica Gajic.

From the Government of the FRY, the prohibition included: Milan Beko, the Minister of Economy, Radmilo Bogdanovic, the Chairman of the Federal Parliament Security Committee, Srđa Bozovic, the President of the Republics' Council, Momir Bulatovic, the President of the Government, Pavle Bulatovic, the Minister of Defense, Branko Crni, the Advisor in the Ministry of Internal Affairs, Velizar Đeric, the Minister of Sport, General-Major Milan Jevtic, the Head of the Administration of the Ministry of Defense, Jugoslav Kostic, the Minister without Portfolio, Zoran Lilic, the Vice-President of the Government, Dragan Markovic, the Minister without Portfolio, Ivan Markovic, the Minister of Telecommunication, Goran Matic, the Minister without Portfolio, Milomir Minic, the President of the Council of Citizens, Tomislav Nikolic, the Deputy President of the Government, Nikola

Sainovic, the Vice-President of the Government, Margit Savovic, the Minister without Portfolio, Zoran Sokolovic, the Minister of Internal Affairs, Borka Vucic, the Minister for the Cooperation with International Financial Organizations, Nebojsa Vujovic, the Spokesman of the Minister of Foreign Affairs, and Jovan Zebic, the Vice-President of the Government.

Bill Clinton was punishing Slobodan Milosevic

From the Serbian Government, the CIA added the following names to the list: Zoran Anđelkovic, the President of the Temporary Executive Council of Kosovo, Milovan Bojic, the Vice-President of the Government, Jovan Damjanovic, the Minister without Portfolio, Vlastimir Djordjevic, the Deputy Minister of Interior, Branislav Ivkovic, the Minister for Science and Technology, Bogoljub Karic, the Minister without Portfolio, Mirko Marjanovic, the President of the Government, Radomir Markovic, the Deputy Minister of Internal Affairs, Milan Milutinovic, the President, Bosko Perosevic, a member of the Executive Council of Vojvodina, Dragisa Ristivojevic, the Assistant of the Head of Public Security, Vojislav Seselj, the Vice President, Frenki Simatovic, the Head of the State Security Special Forces, Zeljko

Simic, the Minister of Culture, Vlajko Stojiljkovic, the Minister of Internal Affairs, Dragan Tomic, the President of the Serbian Parliament and the Director of *Jugopetrol*, Dragomir Tomic, the Vice President of the Government, Aleksandar Vucic, the Minister of Information, Bozidar Vucurovic, the Minister without Portfolio, and Vojislav Zivkovic, a member of the Temporary Executive Council of Kosovo.

From the Yugoslav Army, the list included all commanders, chief officers, and generals, even Dragoljub Ojdanic, the Head of General Staff of the Yugoslav Army, Nebojsa Pavkovic, the Commander of the 3rd Army, Milan Simic, the Head of General Staff for Information and Moral, Spasoje Smiljanic, the Commander of the Air Force and Air Defense, Ljubisa Stojinovic, the Commander of the Special Forces, and the Lieutenant Colonel Todorov, the Commander of the 63rd Airborne Brigade.

The list of people "close to the regime of the President Milosevic", according to the CIA estimates, was comprised of: Slobodan Aćimovic, the Assistant Director of *Beogradska Bank*, Snezana Aleksic, a member of the JUL Directorate, Dragan Antic, the General Manager of *Politika A.D.*, Zoran Aranđelovic, *Nis Tobacco Industry*, Momcilo Babic, the Director of the Medical Center "Bezanijska kosa", Novak Bjelic, the Director of *Kombinat Trepca*, Dragan Bozanic, a member of the JUL Directorate, Radoman Bozovic, the President of *Genex*, Dobrivoje Budimirovic, the President of *Srbijasume*, Jovan Cekovic, the Director of *Jugoimport STDR*, Dusan Cukic, the Foreign Politics Editor of RTS, Ivica Dacic, the Spokesman of SPS, Jevrem Damjanovic, the Main Editor of *Ilustrovana Politika*, Dusan Djordjevic, *Tanjug*, Zivorad Djordjevic, the main editor of *Borba*, Gorica Gajevic, the General Secretary of SPS, Hadzi Dragan Antic, *Politika*, Zivorad Ivic, a member of the Main Board of SPS.

Then, there were: Milanka Karic, the wife of Bogoljub Karic, Sreten Karic, a member of the Karic family, Zoran Karic, a member of the Karic family, Mihalj Kertes, the Director of the Federal Customs Administration, Milorad Komrakov, the Main Editor of the Informative Program of *RTS*, Tatjana Lenard, a member of the JUL Directorate and the Head of the Informative Program of *RTS*, Dusan Matkovic, the Director of *Zelezara Smederevo* and the Vice President of SPS, Zoran Milosevic, the Mayor of Obilic, Milorad Mircic, a representative of the SRS in the Serbian Parliament, Bratislava Morina, the JUL and Serbian Commissioner for Refugees, Milutin Mrkonjic, the Director of *CIP*, Radovan Pankov, a member of the Executive Board of SPS, Goran Percevic, a member of the Executive Board of SPS, Zlatan Perucic, the President of *Beogradska Bank*, Zika Petrovic, the General Manager of *JAT*, Slobodan Radulovic, the General Manager of *C Market*, Ljubisa Ristic, the President of JUL, Dmitar Segrt, the Director of *Toza Markovic*, Lale Sekulic, the former General Manager of the Customs, Radoslav Lale Sekulic, a businessman (he had two criminal records), Jadranka Seselj, the Editor of *Velika Srbija*, Vladimir Stambuk, a member of the JUL Directorate, Rajko Uncanin, the General Manager of *Grmec*, Slobodan Unkovic, the Ambassador of the FRY in China, Milovan Vitezovic, the Main Editor of RTS, Milija Zecevic, a banker, Mirjana Zecevic, the Marketing Manager of the *Politika*.

The list of persons that were "actively helping the regime" included: Oliver Antic, the Dean of the Faculty of Law in Belgrade, Miodrag Babic, the General Manager of *Hemofarm* from Vrsac, Zoran Janaćkovic, the Ambassador of the FRY in Macedonia, Miomir Kalezic, the Commercial Manager of *Jugoimport SDPR*, Đorđe Martic, the Main Editor of the *Politika Ekspres*, Svetozar Milosevic, the nephew of the President of the FRY, Borislav Pelevic, the President of the Serbian Unity Party, and Ratko Vucurovic, the General Manager of *Cable Industry* in Jagodina.

In June 2001, President George Bush signed the Executive Order for the Balkans blocking all property and interests of the persons identified in that Order. The list included more than 150 names of persons and organizations accused by the International Criminal Tribunal for the Former Yugoslavia of materially supporting the accused, as well as those that promoted the institutions that were outside the legal system and which obstructed the peace process in the region.

"The identification of these persons will help in the efforts of international civil and military organizations, as well as domestic authorities in the fight against extremism and in the promotion of stability. In addition to that, the Order for the Western Balkans on the Prohibition of Issuing Visas, from 2001, remains effective," it was said in the statement of the White House in Washington.

The list of people from Serbia included: Mirjana Markovic, Milica Gajic Milosevic, Borislav Milosevic, Marko Milosevic, Milanka Milosevic, Milorad Lukovic Legija, Radovan Markovic, Nebojsa Pavkovic, and Zarko Nikolic.

In the Bush's list, among others, there also were: Dr Radovan Karadzic and his family members, Ratko Mladic, Vojislav Seselj, Ljubo Ćesic Rojs, Valentin Ćoric, Milovan Bjelica, Đojo Arsenovic, and Slavko Roguljic.

When the first black president Barack Obama came to power in the USA, a decision was made to allow Serbian politicians to travel freely to the United States. Only Marko Jaksic, a doctor and a member of DSS from Kosovska Mitrovica remained in the US black list. The US Embassy issued a diplomatic visa to the Deputy Prime Minister Ivica Dacic so that he could travel to the breakfast with the US President Barack Obama.

Slobodan Milosevic and Radovan Karadzic, as Serbian leaders, were travelling around the world with special permissions of the USA, EU, and UN. Milosevic didn't care that his associates weren't allowed to travel anywhere in the West. He was a political chameleon, changing his politics depending on the circumstances in Serbia and the current situation in the international scene. He sacrificed his close associates, especially Radovan Karadzic. He did that because he was forced to fight for his electorate. He was losing control over the people and voters. The organization system of the League of Communists of Yugoslavia and SPS, which were ruling over the company directors, fell apart and the new one wasn't created. Instead of company directors and workers, the political will of Slobodan Milosevic was executed by his sympathizers, party fanatics, corrupt officials, officers, bankers, tycoons, and mobsters. The USA proclaimed them to be dangerous and undesirable Serbs.

Because of the personal greed of Slobodan Milosevic, Mirjana Markovic, and their clique, Serbian people were militarily and politically defeated. Reputable Serbs became detainees of the international community. And, Serbia was turned into an American colony, which was, during the rule of DOS, shredded and robbed, this time, through criminal privatization, by the people who'd got rich by waging the war and state smuggling.

"Rastko Petrovic" Charter for Dr Djordjevic presented by Miodrag Jaksic, the President of the Centre of Emigrants of Serbia, 2017

THE PERSECUTION OF RADOVAN KARADZIC

Slobodan Milosevic was an impudent man and dangerous for Serbs. He used all his close associates, reputable people, the leaders of the Serbs in the republics and Krajinas, just for his selfish purposes. He used a great writer, Dobrica Ćosic, to build up his reputation among people, even for a short while. Ćosic was his first President of the FRY, from June 1992 to June 1993.

When I met Dobrica on one occasion, while he was the President of Yugoslavia, and asked him why he wasn't ruling in accordance with the Constitution, he replied:

"I don't know. I'm a writer. I have no idea why they've put me in this position to rule."

However, the academic and the President, Dobrica Ćosic, did know about the privileges of that position and he asked me:

"Have you brought me Kent Gold for my wife?"

Milosevic politically used and personally exhausted and humiliated Milan Panic, an American businessman, brought by Dusko Mitevic, without the blessing of the White House, to be appointed the first Prime Minister of his new country, the FRY, in 1992. The time has shown that Panic also worked in his own interest. As a real selfish American, Milan Panic gossiped about Slobodan Milosevic in front of me and the Americans. He tried to deceive Milosevic and turn the USA against the Serbian archon. Panic was removed from his position, but, unlike Dobrica Ćosic, he first got filthy rich in Serbia. He bought the drug factory *INC Galenika,* sold medicines in Russia, and earned billions.

Jimmy and Rosalynn Carter with Borko in Pale in 1994

And, while Milan Panic was an egomaniac, Dobrica Ćosic just a political profiteer, a stale dissident, and a great Serb with a Communist pedigree, my friend and an academic, Ljubisa Rakic was a real critic of Slobodan Milosevic. Slobodan Milosevic banished Milan Panic and Dobrica Ćosic away from him and the power, and then, he ordered his thugs to beat up Ljubisa Rakic because he willfully abandoned the Serbian archon. I personally treated the wounds of the academic Rakic, the President of SANU (Serbian Academy of Science and Art), inflicted by Slobodan Milosevic's men.

As a politician, President Slobodan Milosevic exhibited his violent nature most towards Radovan Karadzic, the leader of Bosnian Serbs. I witnessed Slobodan Milosevic expressing enormous hatred toward Dr Karadzic during 1994, while I was the envoy of the Republic of Srpska in the USA. That year, Milosevic was still at the political war with Washington. The Americans described him as the President of the FRY and the leader of all the Serbs in the Balkans. They chose Dr Radovan Karadzic to become the new Serbian archon. In order to show their trust to Karadzic, President Bill Clinton and the State Department authorized the former US President Jimmy Carter to visit Pale and reach peace in Bosnia. I was the main organizer of this historic meeting that ended in December 1994 by signing a peace agreement among Serbs, Croats, and Muslims in Bosnia and Herzegovina. The peace lasted for four and a half months.

Jealous of the strengthening of Karadzic's political position in the Balkans and the USA, the archon Milosevic started a war against the President of the Republic of Srpska.

Jimmy Carter, Radovan Karadzic, and Borko Djordjevic in Pale in 1994

The conflict of Slobodan Milosevic and Radovan Karadzic was an epic and historic argument, a political battle of two great Serbs, not for the status and fate of the Serbian people, but for their own personal interests. Each of them fought for himself. As statesmen and leaders, neither Slobodan Milosevic, nor Radovan Karadzic had a system of work or a vision of their own, national and state progress. Both of them acted as real Serbian haiduks. They planned for just one day at the time. They never thought much about the future.

Americans truly respected Radovan Karadzic, because they, generally, respect the winners. And, in 1994, Karadzic ruled over 72%of the territory of Bosnia and Herzegovina. Nevertheless, as they respect winners, Americans don't respect losers. And, Radovan Karadzic disappointed Americans and became a loser.

What happened?

Vojislav Seselj, as the para-military commander and Jovica Stanisic, as the Head of the Serbian Secret Police, then Arkan's *Tigers* and

Seselj's *White Eagles* were always with Radovan and in Pale. By that, they intentionally created the impression with the Americans that the Republic of Srpska had become the militant center of Serbdom. Owing to that defamation, Radovan started losing his reputation and legitimacy in the United States. Thus, Americans started leaving Karadzic out of all political options. However, Jimmy Carter believed Karadzic was an honest man and that he was better for peace and Serbs than Milosevic. He estimated that Radovan Karadzic wasn't a dangerous Serb and that Slobodan Milosevic was quite dangerous, even calamitous for the Serbs.

Karadzic was terrified of Milosevic. Whenever Milosevic phoned and criticized him, Karadzic would go pale, bite his fingernails, and pull his hair. Milosevic threatened to take his army, to forbid him to come to Belgrade, to reveal his card gambling affairs. Slobodan criticized Radovan, threatened him, pushed him away, but Karadzic always returned to him and meekly approached him. That is why Jimmy Carter, sensing that Milosevic would crush Karadzic, sent a warning to Radovan in 1995, when he heard that the leader of the Bosnian Serbs would go to Belgrade to meet Slobodan Milosevic and the Patriarch Pavle:

"Don't go to Belgrade. The meeting with Milosevic is a great scam!He's going to kill you!"

Carter informed me personally that if Karadzic went to Serbia, NATO would bombard Pale, acting by the orders of Richard Holbrooke, Clinton's envoy for Bosnia and Herzegovina and, also, an associate of Milosevic. And, that is exactly what happened on 30th August 1995. The moment Radovan crossed the Drina River near Loznica, at 2 a.m., NATO attacked Pale. Bombs were dropped on all the state buildings of the Republic of Srpska. The personal secretary of Karadzic, Jovan Zametica, was drunk with fear. I hid in the cellar of the Hotel *Bistrica*. I had sent my underaged daughter Aleksandra Djordjevic to Belgrade and saved her life.

There, in a shelter in Pale, I found out that two Spaniards from the Contact Group were instructing the bombers towards the capital city of Srpska, Pale, and the house of Radovan Karadzic. Officially, NATO attacked the Republic of Srpska because of the massacre at Markale market in Sarajevo, when, on 28th August, 37 civilians were allegedly killed by Serbian mortar shells. By

14th September, NATO dropped 10,000 tons of ammunition and explosives with depleted uranium on Bosnian Serbs.

The news that "Serbian bombs" killed dozens of Muslims at Markale market in Sarajevo was an American warning to Radovan Karadzic that he didn't know how to decipher. Instead of apologizing to the Muslims and dismissing his Sarajevo Commander, he ordered the RS Army and the RSK Army to unite into one Serbian army. Milosevic broke that plan into pieces.

I telephoned Radovan and told him that Jimmy Carter advised him to give a statement via CNN and say that he had dismissed the Sarajevo Commander and that he was apologizing to the Muslims, in order to preserve his reputation. In Loznica, the *CNN* crew was waiting for Karadzic, but Radovan didn't give a statement. Radovan didn't listen to his only American friend, Jimmy Carter, but he quickly and easily capitulated in front of Slobodan Milosevic.

Jimmy Carter, Gerald Ford, Richard Nixon, Ronald Reagan and George H. W. Bush with their wives

THE ROTTEN US PRESIDENT

Milosevic blackmailed Karadzic and pushed him away, so that he could impose himself as the only negotiator on the Serbian side. He was secretly discussing peace with Richard Holbrooke in Tito's summerhouse in Karađorđevo. The rotten Jew, Ambassador Richard Holbrooke neutralized all the activities of Radovan Karadzic when he obtained the authorization from Bill Clinton to invite the Serbs to Dayton for peace negotiations. Holbrooke decided to invite Milosevic, although he knew he couldn't go to Dayton without the consent of Radovan Karadzic.

Richard Holbrooke was dealing with the Bosnian Serbs via Carter's Center. At the end of August 1995, he agreed to visit Pale and involve Radovan Karadzic into the peace process on condition that the leader of the Bosnian Serbs respected the requests of the Muslims. Namely, after reaching an agreement between the Serbs and the Muslims, the Americans were supposed to enthrone Radovan Karadzic as the leader of all the Serbs in the Balkans. The Americans had estimated that Karadzic was a softer politician than Slobodan Milosevic, that he could be "worked with" and that the leader of the Bosnian Serbs was ready to make concessions in order to reach his goal, which was the international acceptance and recognition of the Republic of Srpska as an independent country.

While Slobodan Milosevic was advocating for the creation of independent Bosnia and Herzegovina, Radovan Karadzic was fighting for the formation of one country – Bosnia and Herzegovina and the other country – the Republic of Srpska.

Richard Holbrooke brought Yugoslav leaders to Dayton

Slobodan Milosevic officially asked Ambassador Richard Holbrooke to be the one to represent all the Serbs in the Balkans, claiming that Radovan Karadzic was an insurgent who wouldn't listen to him. Holbrooke, who sided with Milosevic, ordered the attack of NATO bombers at the Republic of Srpska and forced Radovan Karadzic to sign a document known as the *Patriarch Agreement* with Slobodan Milosevic.

Then, the US Ambassador Richard Holbrooke personally signed an agreement with Karadzic in which the President of the Republic of Srpska abdicated from power and went into a political retirement, during which the USA promised him a peaceful life. After that, Holbrooke offered Ratko Mladic, as a "brave military leader" to become a politician and take the power from Radovan Karadzic, as well as the leadership over the Serbian part of Bosnia.

Knowing all that, Karadzic went to Belgrade, convinced he would win the country status of the Republic of Srpska in the USA and the international community, and that he would go to the peace negotiations in Dayton. Radovan Karadzic was certain that this endeavor of his would be supported by the Serbian Patriarch Pavle, who had also been invited to the negotiation meeting with Slobodan Milosevic. That is why Karadzic replied to all Carter's and my warnings that Milosevic would attack him by saying:

"I'm going. Milosevic won't dare attack me in front of Patriarch Pavle!"

What Karadzic didn't know was that Milosevic had the Head of the Serbian Orthodox Church (SPC) under his thumb and that he was squeezing him. He was confiscating his import of wax for making candles, which the SPC had a significant pro it from. Milosevic threatened Patriarch Pavle to take the Church away from him and that, without the SPC, he wouldn't be able to protect the Serbian people.

Radovan went straight into Slobodan Milosevic's trap. He stood in front of an array of the archon's generals and the obedient Patriarch Pavle. Both of them, Radovan and Patriarch Pavle, were actually the captives of Slobodan Milosevic, without even knowing that. Karadzic was taken from Belgrade to Dobanovci, where he was practically imprisoned until he put his signature at the authorization for the Dayton Agreement. With that signature, Radovan Karadzic gave Slobodan Milosevic not only his approval to represent the Republic of Srpska at the peace negotiations in Dayton, but, in fact, the right to trade with the Americans and to hand Brcko, Tuzla, Gorazde, and 2% of the Serbian territory in Bosnia and Herzegovina to the Bosnians. In that way, Radovan Karadzic lost control and command over the Republic of Srpska in Dayton and, instead of becoming the leader of all Serbs, he became the greatest Serbian loser.

On the wings of that success, Richard Holbrooke prepared the peace initiative and truce on 5th October 1995. That led to the peak of the US politics, the Dayton Summit, where Richard Holbrooke practically kept captive Slobodan Milosevic, Alija Izetbegovic, and occasionally Franjo Tuđman during November, until they completed the negotiations on the peace agreement and signed the contract that ended the war in the former Yugoslavia.

The negotiations lasted for seventeen days. After them, the post-Dayton Bosnia and Herzegovina was created. The Republic of Srpska was recognized as a political entity, and Bosnia and Herzegovina as an independent country. The Serbs, who ruled over 72% of its territory, got 49% of it, and Croatians and Muslims took 51%.

After the Dayton Agreement, Slobodan Milosevic, from the "Butcher of the Balkans" and the last Communist dictator, became the favorite stability factor in the Balkans, practically overnight.

Richard Holbrooke was really delighted by him. They had feasts and fun, and he didn't have time for the Serbian opposition. But, Milosevic completely mistakenly estimated his real importance and role. Holbrooke went to negotiations with Milosevic fraught with prejudice. He was quite surprised when he met neither a communist nor a nationalist nor even an Oriental dictator. He was facing a man who was absolutely nothing of the kind.

Milosevic wasn't a victim of an ideology, or any principle, except that the fact that, as every other opportunist, he used them relentlessly to defend his power. Holbrooke even found him quite charming in his honesty and callousness.

Not even at one point, did Sloba protect Radovan Karadzic and the Serbian people in Bosnia and Herzegovina. He sold Karadzic to Ambassador Holbrooke. He defamed him in front of the Americans as a bad person and a terrible politician. On the other hand, Milosevic strived to charm and win over Holbrooke at any cost. He didn't suspect he would be tricked at the end of the bravura performance in which he was the main star for a brief moment.

Milosevic requested from Karadzic to retreat the Serbian army from Bihać. He was convinced the US bombs had curative power over the hot-headed Serbs in Bosnia. Richard Holbrooke bragged to his associates about how kindly Milosevic welcomed him while NATO was bombing Bosnian Serbs. He thought Milosevic would reject to see him and tell him to go back where he'd come from.

"Dick, I have splendid news for you!" Slobodan approached to greet him and gave him a hug, which quite confused him.

The moment they met, he pulled out the paper with the authorization of the leadership of Bosnian Serbs stating that he, Slobodan Milosevic, could negotiate in Dayton over the peace agreement in Bosnia on the behalf of Radovan Karadzic. Holbrooke couldn't refrain from expressing his astonishment by Milosevic welcoming him in such an affable manner at the moment when US bombs were being relentlessly dropped on the Serbs in Bosnia.

"What's so astonishing about that? Dick, they needed to be bombed a little, to get them come to their senses. They are all tremendously pig-headed and hot-headed."

Historical events have shown that Milosevic didn't need the Serbs in Croatia, Bosnia and Herzegovina, Montenegro, and diaspora. He used to say that to the Americans, and at secret meetings with Radovan Karadzic and Dr Jovan Raskovic, he would say:

"You, the Serbs from outside Serbia, stay where you are. Don't touch my Serbia!"

"We don't want to be with Muslims and Croats! We want to be together with Serbia," they would reply.

Milosevic then "sold and delivered" all of them to Alija Izetbegovic and Franjo Tuđman. He falsely represented himself as the leader of all the Serbs in order to remain on power. He just acted to be a great Serb, by sending weapons, his commanders, and para-military and para-police formations to Bosnia and Herzegovina and Croatia. He claimed to the Americans he knew nothing about that.

In that fateful 1995, both Milosevic and Karadzic were hot-headed -the former for defeating his least favorite Serb, and the latter for being defeated by his most favorite Serb. Both of them were so preoccupied with their personal fight for power that they didn't notice they were losing their country.

And, while the Serbs were triumphantly waiting for someone to recognize their victory, the Muslim and Croatian army quickly consolidated. Milosevic adhered incomparably more to the secret agreement with Tuđman and was ready to sacrifice the territories in Bosnia and Krajina for the promised peace and lifting of sanctions.

On the 5th August 1995, the Croatian action *Storm* ensued, and, with the US support, the Serbs were exiled from Krajina and there was a significant danger they might lose Banjaluka, as well.

A political analyst from Washington, Obrad Kesic, wrote in his notes that Richard Holbrooke boasted that he had personally prevented Banjaluka from falling into the hands of Croats, after the *Storm*. It is interesting that, during one closed meeting, Holbrooke revealed that he had indirectly suggested to Milosevic that he had the US permission to attack the Croats and the Muslims:

"Mr President, it wouldn't be good if Banjaluka fell! That wouldn't be in your best interest, and it wouldn't even be in our best interest, because it would cause new conflicts and postpone the peace solution, which is already in sight," Holbrooke said to President Slobodan Milosevic.

Having seen that Milosevic wouldn't do a thing, the Americans were forced to restrain and stop Tuđman in his triumphant victorious march and save Banjaluka from the Croatian occupation in August 1995.

Milosevic was the US favorite for almost two years because he conducted everything Bill Clinton and Richard Holbrooke had ordered him to. And, he literally could do anything he wanted against the so-called internal enemy, i.e. the Serbian opposition. That is why Milosevic recklessly cheated at the local elections in 1997 – because he considered he had the US approval and permission to that. He relied on the silver-tongued messages of the Charge d'Affaires in Washington, Nebojsa Vujovic, saying that the United States was full of admiration and gratitude towards him and his historic mission. On the day the

NATO bombing of Serbia started, on 24th March 1999, he informed him that it would certainly not happen. However, the NATO attack did happen and during the 78 days of the war with the USA and Europe, the Serbian people were politically and militarily defeated in Serbia, as well.

That is why it's no coincidence that Kucan, Tuđman, and Izetbegovic, who weren't up to his knees when political deceptions are concerned, did incomparably more for their peoples than Milosevic. When he thought he'd truly become an inevitable partner of the great powers, Milosevic couldn't realize that he had definitely played his part – *giving everything in return for nothing.*

It's a paradox that Milosevic had a considerably stronger negotiating position when he was the Butcher of the Balkans and held one third of Croatia and 72% of Bosnia under his control than when he recklessly ceded – *in order to be affectionately named the Stability Factor of the Balkans.*

He may have not fulfilled Serbian national interests, but he certainly did carry out the American ones. He definitely brought the USA to the Balkans, though perhaps against its will, and provided a completely new life to NATO, after the bombardment of Serbia.

As Obrad Kesic claims, and I agree with him, Milosevic wasn't an American man, as he would sometimes say for himself. Milosevic mostly disseminated the story that he knew what he was doing and that it was all a part of a great world strategy. Not until he'd lost everything, did it become clear that it was all just a bluff and self-deceit, by which he irreparably destroyed Serbian national interests and let down the US interests in Yugoslavia.

When a cowboy pulls a gun, he doesn't brandish it, but shoots from it. The USA doesn't make empty threats and it is usually compelled to use force. The Americans appreciate only absolutely obedient politicians and their allies. Milosevic tried to deceive them and they punished him with his death in the Hague prison.

THE TRAP FOR THE ARCHON

During the rule of Bill Clinton, the USA officially evaluated the President of Serbia as an unpredictable politician. The CIA gave such an estimate to Richard Holbrooke when he was going to Belgrade to negotiate with Slobodan Milosevic. Holbrooke succeeded in agreeing with the President of Serbia on the terms for generating peace in Croatia and in Bosnia and Herzegovina, for signing the Erdut Agreement and the Dayton Agreement, i.e. for the return of Krajina and Slavonia under the wing of Croatia.

In the US administration, the defeat of the Serbs from Krajina in the summer of 1995 was directly linked with Slobodan Milosevic, Serbia and the Yugoslav Army, which remained neutral. This move of President Slobodan Milosevic clearly stated that he had decided to sever all ties with the Serbs from Krajina and, thereby, to leave the "western Serbs" to their fate. With this move, Milosevic put the internal stability of the country under risk. It was certainly shaken with the in low of dozens of thousand refugees, as well as with the potential national rage, caused by the obvious collective humiliation. The events in Krajina influenced Washington to move into an aggressive action in Bosnia. Regardless of the fact that the instructions of government institutions and agencies, the Pentagon and the CIA, increasingly involved the USA into the Bosnian nightmare, the faith in military intervention continued to grow.

Holbrooke's trap for Milosevic

Bill Clinton and his associates estimated that Slobodan Milosevic was an ideal politician to cooperate with and Serbia seemed to be the best ally for the Balkan peace.

When he completed his political and espionage mission in the Balkans, Ambassador Richard Holbrooke became the US representative in the UN. He wrote memoires *To End a War* and admitted in them that it was much easier for him to persuade Slobodan Milosevic than Radovan Karadzic.

"Warren Christopher and I concluded that we should negotiate only with Milosevic and that he should be held accountable for the actions of Bosnian Serbs."

The US intelligence officer Maarten Van Hoven publicly spoke about that. His text, published in a reputable Washington magazine *Foreign Policy* in 1995, was the first reliable indication of the U-turn of Clinton's administration and opting for Serbia as the backbone of the future Balkan politics.

In that context, Slobodan Milosevic was, at least temporarily, an ally the USA counted on. Hoven wrote:

"No matter what scenario is foreseen for Serbia during the next two to five years, it will be a key force in the Balkans owing to its central position, newly acquired territories, Serbian ethnic cohesion, cultural spirit, military capacities, and energetic and unyielding leadership. Serbia would inevitably exercise a hegemonic influence. Additionally, Serbia still has friends in Moscow. With the right set of circumstances, it could also refer to the historical bonds with Great Britain and France. Considering the power of Serbia and the relative weakness of its neighbors, Serbian influence in the region that used to be Yugoslavia and around it will be quite significant."

At the same time, the USA was preparing the indictment for war crimes against Milosevic, in case he tricked Washington, as he had done at the beginning of 1992. That indictment was written by Ambassador Warren Zimmermann and sent to the White House.

Rejecting any accountability of the USA for the Yugoslav catastrophe, Zimmermann had accusatory comments for all the republics and their leaders, most of all for Milosevic, who he personally couldn't stand:

"As the court of history pursues its investigation of the death of Yugoslavia, I can imagine the following indictments: Slovenia for selfishness toward its fellow Yugoslavs; Tudjman's Croatia for insensitivity toward its Serbian population and greed toward its Bosnian neighbors; the Yugoslav army for ideological rigidity and arrogance, culminating in war crimes; Radovan Karadzic for attacking the principle of tolerance in Yugoslavia's most ethnically mixed republic; and— most of all—Slobodan Milosevic for devising and pursuing a strategy that led directly to the breakup of the country and to the deaths of over a hundred thousand of its citizens. Nationalism was the arrow that killed Yugoslavia. Milosevic was the principal bowman. The Serbian leader made Yugoslavia intolerable for anybody who wasn't a Serb. He is hated among Albanians, Slovenes, Croats, Muslims, Macedonians, and Hungarians. And he has brought his own people into poverty and despair. Milosevic's dream of 'all Serbs in one state' is a nightmare today; Serbs are now scattered among four states—'Yugoslavia' (Serbia and Montenegro), Bosnia, Croatia, and Macedonia. In seeking to dominate Yugoslavia, Milosevic destroyed it.

In seeking to tear out the pieces where Serbs lived, he wrecked, for a generation or more, the future of all Serbs."

After the meeting with Milosevic and after the massacre in Srebrenica, Richard Holbrooke wrote about the Archon stating that he had committed "the worst war crimes in Europe since the Holocaust". In that manner, Holbrooke was persuading Washington to put additional pressure on Milosevic and to push the Serbs out of the political arrangement on the division within the former Yugoslavia.

The main problem of the Americans, Bill Clinton himself, and the US administration was that they couldn't ind a suitable replacement for Slobodan Milosevic. Nobody was so obedient and so powerful as Milosevic. Vuk Draskovic seemed politically too small, even though he had the Serbian Renewal Movement (SPO) with a million of its members to support him. Dragoljub Micunovic didn't suit them because he politically wavered too much. Vojislav Seselj was too dangerous with his nationalistic ideas. And, Zoran Đindic was never an option because of his pro-European orientation and because he stood by Radovan Karadzic when he was rejected by the official Belgrade and Slobodan Milosevic. That is why, in spring 1995, the USA decided to support Slobodan Milosevic, the man they least wanted for an ally. Washington was also incited to do so by the report of the Commission on the Balkans of the Carnegie Endowment and the Aspen Institute Berlin created after the visit to Serbia and Belgrade during 1996. Among other things, that report says the following on Serbia and Milosevic:

"The priorities for Serbia in the following period are: (1) national re-examination; (2) political democracy; (3) rule of law, and (4) market economy. Milosevic most likely won't bring these changes. Milosevic's political ability stems from an instinctive pragmatism that enables him to take up or shed options not when, but before it becomes essential to do so. In Serbia itself, he had been doing this since mid-1980s. Since 1994, he has applied the approach with extraordinary success in the international field. He saw defeats coming and accommodated them by refashioning himself as a peacemaker. In doing so, he gained an aura of indispensability. To be sure, Milosevic made an important contribution to Dayton. He used the Dayton negotiations to save himself and he seems to have succeeded in that."

Both the Americans and the Europeans estimated at the time that Milosevic's political superiority within the FRY and

Bosnia and Herzegovina was unbeatable, but that his future was completely uncertain. Such warning was written in the report of the Commission on the Balkans of the Carnegie Endowment at the end of 1996:

"Milosevic's position, however, might not be so certain in the future as it seems at the moment. His Socialist Party of Serbia is far less powerful than himself. It has a small majority advantage in the Assembly and it can form the Government only with a support of a fraction. Milosevic is, also, facing the constitutional issue and two possible solutions of his political dilemma – Serbia or Yugoslavia. Current administrative units – Serbia, Montenegro, Kosovo, and Vojvodina – are politically non-uniform and non-functional. Milosevic will soon have to show all his resourcefulness in order to retain the power in the FRY."

The ostensible US support to Milosevic from 1994 was actually a deadly trap for the Serbian archon. The USA still treated him as the enemy of the state and a dangerous person. CNN incessantly denounced him for the committed war crimes in the territory of the FRY and the official Washington called him a dictator. When Milosevic was accepted as a Yugoslav peacemaker, after the signing of the Dayton Peace Agreement in December 1995, the European Union suspended the sanctions towards the FRY. However, the USA retained the so-called "outer wall" of sanctions towards Serbia and Montenegro in order to punish and blackmail the FRY in that manner. At the beginning of 1996, the US Charge d'Affaires, Richard Miles publicly spoke about that in the middle of Belgrade. He simply listed what the USA expected Yugoslavia to do in order to be a free country:

"Until the Federal Republic of Yugoslavia meets the following criteria, it won't be allowed the following: to participate in the work of the UN and other international organizations; to join the IMF, the World Bank, or other international financial institutions; to normalize its bilateral relations with the United States. First of all, we seek the improvement of the situation in Kosovo. Secondly, we insist on the full cooperation of the Serbian government in locating and arresting all persons suspected of war crimes in order to bring them in front of the Hague Tribunal. Let us notice that the four suspected persons, including the so-called Vukovar Three, accused by the Hague Tribunal, are still at large in Serbia and Montenegro. Thirdly, we demand progress in the resolution of the matter of public heritage with other republics of former Yugoslavia. Apart from resolving these issues, the Unites States are quite interested in the democratization process in this country, which involves the opening of media, as well. Because of the significant interest, the crisis in Serbia caused in the USA, and because we believe that the democratic changes in Serbia are in the interest of stability in the region, the US administration and the Congress are particularly interested in the development of democratic institutions in Serbia and Montenegro during the following months," concluded Richard Miles.

At the beginning of November 1996, the United Nations Security Council Resolution 1074 was adopted terminating the sanctions against the FRY. The termination of all the sanctions was conditioned by the obligation of Serbia and Montenegro to make a progress in Kosovo and Metohija, to cooperate with the Hague Tribunal, and to resolve the issues of state heritage with other former Yugoslav republics. As that wasn't accomplished, in 1998, sanctions were re-introduced in the FR of Yugoslavia, this time by the EU and the USA, due to the accusations for the persecution of Albanians from Kosovo and Metohija and for the excessive use of force during the war in this province.

Although the war in Kosovo and Metohija ended in June 1999, the sanctions of the international community against the Serbian people and country were lifted only when Slobodan Milosevic was removed from power, in October 2000.

THE MANHUNTS

Nowadays, many people speak about the way Slobodan Milosevic awoke Serbdom in former Communists and Yugoslavs, the way he resisted the new world order and the domination of the USA and NATO, and made Serbia a democratic country. That is true, but the Serbian people paid a considerable and bloody price for that. The Serbs first became the hostages of Slobodan Milosevic and his wife Mirjana Markovic, and then, their victims.

Milosevic, with his clique, turned public media into the ground for spreading international hatred towards everything that wasn't Serbian. He became the leader of the joint criminal venture. The YNA and the Serbian Army of Milosevic conducted aggression over Croatia and Bosnia and Herzegovina. His soldiery, including the criminals Arkan and Legija, started a bloody war against the civilians of the non-Serbian origin. His military and para-military formations opened concentration camps, ethnically cleansed entire areas, organized rapes. Their war crimes occurred every day. Milosevic's army and police exiled hundreds of thousands of Albanians from Kosovo and caused the exodus of around 300,000 Kosmet Serbs. Milosevic fought tooth and nail to cause the NATO intervention knowing that it would definitely turn the citizens of Serbia away from the Western world. He transformed Serbia into the prison for all the nations.

Along the way, he robbed the citizens of his beloved Serbia, seizing their old foreign exchange savings and pension fund, and calling for the Loan for Economic Revival of Serbia without the intention to return the money. He launched a vortex of destruction that sucked all the segments of society. He caused moral, economic, political, and physical devastation of historic proportions that Serbia still hasn't recovered from.

Serbs in Kosmet

With his relentless propaganda, he poisoned entire generations and those offering the antidote are still considered traitors, mercenaries, and, as Milosevic would put it, "domicile good-for-nothings".

While he was getting ready to sign the Dayton Agreement and while he was negotiating the peace in Kosovo, Milosevic continued conducting political violence in Bosnia and Serbia. He was waging a civil war that the Serbian people didn't want.

Instead of dealing with terrorists and armed Albanian separatists, who were helped by both the USA and Russia, Milosevic ordered the attack at the Albanian civilians in Kosmet. He mobilized Serbs and took them to Kosmet to wage war. Many mobilized Serbs understood that as a call to war for the liberation of the country of "Arnauts", and many as a call for robbing Albanians and Serbs in Kosmet. The war of Milosevic's Serbs with the Albanians was actually a great robbery of the people from Kosovo. Serbia was, once again, criminalized and turned into the country of organized criminal groups. Many Serbian military units were comprised of patriots, who honorably and bravely fought against the Albanian terrorists, but also of criminals who robbed the houses of Albanians and Serbs on that front.

A group of mobilized men from the territory of Leposavic Municipality, for instance, drove a tractor to the front with them so that they could load the stolen goods on it. That is how some war profiteers were created and they, upon their return home, in their towns and municipalities throughout Serbia, opened cafes, restaurants, exchange of ices, hostels, etc. They became new Serbian businessmen, sponsors of political parties and their functionaries, as well as the lords of Serbian provinces.

It is a well-known fact that, during the civil war in the FRY from 1990 to 1995, Serbs were killed in Slovenia, Croatia, Bosnia and Herzegovina, Montenegro, and Serbia. What is worse, with his national politics, which can now be characterized as the politics of deceit, Milosevic ruined young Serbian generations, because he was leading them into wars which they lost and in which they were killed. That is the greatest Serbian national embarrassment which the Serbian Army and the Ministry of Internal Affairs of Serbia are silent about, because they were accomplices in this crime.

It is not such a well-known fact, because it is kept a secret, how Milosevic's squadrons of military police and police from Serbia, but also from Krajina and Bosnia, conducted their manhunts. People from Belgrade, Novi Sad, Nis, Leskovac, and other Serbian towns were apprehended, under the pretext of war mobilization, and violently taken to the fronts in other countries – Bosnia and Herzegovina and Croatia. According to the data of the Democrats of Vojvodina, during these manhunts, around 200,000 young men were mobilized.

The greatest hunt for recruits was conducted in 1995. Then, the police of Serbia, the police of the Republic of Srpska, and the members of Arkan's Volunteer Guard, supported by the Ministry of Internal Affairs, were arresting all the Serbian residents that were born or had origins in Croatia or Bosnia and Herzegovina, as well as the men born in Serbia, but who were against the war. With the use of police torture, the men were arrested in their homes, workplaces, students' hostels, in the streets. Policemen and Arkan's men were cruel, insolent, and sarcastic. They would ask their captives:

"'d you like to war a bit?"

"I would!"

"Take him to dig trenches in Bosnia!"

Forcibly mobilized men in Belgrade were taken to custody in the "White House", which was the police building in Karaburma. From there, they were taken in a police van to the police station in Milana Rakica Street. There, being named "deserters and Serbian embarrassments", they were recruited.

The indictment against the "deserters" was written by none the other but Dr Mira Markovic in her columns in *Duga* magazine, where she hinted at the police hunts of Belgrade residents:

"One part of fighters for the Serbian cause in Bosnia and Serbian Krajina live in Belgrade, without spending a day in the war and without even planning to. They mostly came from the regions where there's war and they did it on time, just before the war started or during its first days. They came to Belgrade, but also to the other towns in Serbia, with their children, with their money, and with their ambitions – to take over economic, political, and social positions in general, which will make them the first-class citizens, above any category..."

The daily *Politika*, the main media of Slobodan Milosevic during that time, wrote with approval about the arrests of civilians and the forcible mobilization: *"The men from Krajina are coming to help. The buses crowded with military conscripts and volunteers from Serbia are arriving in the RSK."*

On their way to Bosnia, the gathering place of the mobilized was in Karakaj near Zvornik, in an abandoned production hall. The men arrested in the capital city were called "the Belgrade Troop". In Zvornik, they were deployed in the 2nd Krajina Sarajevo Corps. They were taken by bus to Pale, where they were lined up and guarded by armed policemen, who addressed them as "Cattle!"

In the summer of 1995, the arrested men from Belgrade were transferred in a military truck to Ilidza, via Vogosća and Railovac, and placed in the hall of the *Jadran* Hotel. There, they had a lecture on desertion. The forcibly mobilized were deployed on Igman, the locality of Sugreb. Their headquarters on Igman was in the hotel *Srbija*, the rooms of which were destroyed and looted, without water and electricity. At the end of June 1995, the captives were given weapons and taken to the position on Igman. There were underaged fighters among them – children and older minors. The Muslims that had them at gunpoint, would tell them:

"Belgraders, go back home! Bosnia is not for you!"

The parents of the forcibly mobilized men on the front could get some information on them from the Bureau of the Government of the Republic of Srpska in Belgrade. There were 7,000 arrested and forcibly mobilized men from Belgrade. The permission for a free weekend from Bosnia and Herzegovina or Croatia to Serbia cost them 500 German marks. If they had remained in Belgrade, they would have been caught again and forcibly returned to the front. The ones who gave 2,000 German marks would be left to stay in Belgrade and they would avoid the forced warring. Those men would become smugglers, supplying the fighters with cigarettes and tranquilizers, which the soldiers called "Zunza".

The forcibly mobilized and their relatives would secretly wonder why Marija Milosevic, the daughter of Slobodan and Mira, who was good at shooting, didn't go to war. Why her brother, Marko Milosevic, who was trained to shoot from an automatic rifle by police officers in the shooting alley in Sarajevska Street, wasn't mobilized?

The children of the Serbian Archon were forbidden by their parents to die for the Serbian people. They waged their war in media, because Marija was spreading the Yugoslavhood over her radio station Kosava, and on the black market, where Marko was dealing with cigarettes and foreign exchange. That is how Slobodan Milosevic, in the middle of the war, once again criminalized Serbia and ruined its young people.

THE SECRETS OF DAYTON

The Dayton Peace Agreement was reached in the Wright-Patterson Air Force Base near Dayton, in the US state Ohio. The conference lasted from 1st to 21st November 1995. The main participants were the then President of Serbia Slobodan Milosevic, the President of the Republic of Bosnia and Herzegovina Alija Izetbegovic, the President of Croatia Franjo Tuđman, the US Mediator Richard Holbrooke, and General Wesley Clark. The Serbs from Bosnia and Herzegovina didn't have their direct representatives.

With this Agreement, the war in Bosnia and Herzegovina ended, having lasted from 1992 to 1995. According to this Agreement, Bosnia and Herzegovina was divided into two parts: the Muslim-Croatian Federation with 51% and the Republic of Srpska with 49% of the territory. The city of Brcko in Bosanska Posavina obtained a special status, while the city of Neum at the Adriatic Sea is supposed to become a part of the Republic of Croatia in 2095.

The signing of the Dayton Agreement in Paris

The Agreement was officially signed in Paris on 14th December. The Assembly of the FRY ratified the agreement on 21st November 2002. That document not only established peace in this region, but it also normalized the relations among the nations. In the military Annex of that Agreement, the countries committed to limit their armament and to reduce the number of soldiers under the international supervision. The Agreement consists of twenty documents, referring to the inter-ethnic borders, military aspect of the peace solution, the NATO status in Bosnia and Herzegovina, Croatia, and FRY, regional stability, human rights in Bosnia and Herzegovina, refugees, internally displaced persons, and the creation of the Federation in Bosnia and Herzegovina.

The Dayton Agreement was the culmination of the socalled shuttle diplomacy initiated by Richard Holbrooke with his team, under the auspices of the USA. The *New York Times* wrote that the negotiations on Bosnia functioned because Richard Holbrooke knew that the Balkans was the snakes' pit, so he had decided to be a "python" in that pit. In Dayton, Richard Holbrooke cursed, shouted, and pounded his fist on the table because Izetbegovic and Milosevic refused to put their signatures on the paper.

Holbrooke succeeded in Dayton not only because he knew how to roar and pound his fist on the table, but because, behind that fist, there was the most powerful country in the world and because the conflicting sides were forced to make compromises. He yelled at Sacirbey, Buha, Koljevic, Milosevic... He blackmailed the Yugoslav leaders because he knew all their private and political secrets. Without their knowing that, he secretly persuaded Milosevic, Izetbegovic, and Tuđman to put their signatures on the document, offering them the US dollars and the support of President Bill Clinton, personally, as a reward.

Holbrooke himself spoke that those were the most difficult negotiations of the contemporary diplomacy, but also "the moment of the birth of the new world politics after the Cold War".

However, Holbrooke behaved as a serpent in that mission. Secretly and without the White House knowing it, he sent his own son, Phyllis Oakley, in an espionage action. He sent to the US Government, Pentagon, and the CIA a report from Srebrenica and Zepa "where in July 1995, the Serbs massacred thousands of people surrounded in the UN protection zones," while the UN peace-keeping units stood there helpless.

Serbian leaders from Croatia and Bosnia and Herzegovina considered, and so do I, that Milosevic betrayed the Serbs from Krajina and Slavonia in Dayton. Before signing the Peace Agreement, Milosevic had arranged with Tuđman the manner of dividing Bosnia and Herzegovina, so that the Serbs would get the Republic of Srpska and that he returned to the Croatians the Serbian parts of Krajina and Slavonia, but without Serbs. The military operations of the Croatian Army – *Storm* and *Flash* were a part of Milosevic-Tuđman agreement, with the support of the US Airforce, to exile the Serbs from Krajina and

Slavonia, i.e. from Croatia. When, on 5th August 1995, the exodus of Serbs from Croatia started, Milosevic's state television didn't broadcast that news. It was silent about that embarrassment of Milosevic for several hours.

In Dayton, under the control of Richard Holbrooke and the USA, Milosevic betrayed both Radovan Karadzic and the Bosnian Serbs. He seized the land ownership and Serbian territories from Bosnian Serbs and handed them to Croatians and Muslims. That is why it can be said that Bill Clinton and Richard Holbrook completely defeated Slobodan Milosevic in the US military base in Dayton. The Serbian Archon did what the Americans had expected him to do – reduced the territorial and living space of the Serbs in former Yugoslavia. Milosevic could now create the so-called Great Serbia, which he was constantly accused of, just in Belgrade and its surroundings.

Holbrooke admitted that Dayton wasn't lawless, but it was the best that could have been achieved in the Balkans. The war operations were stopped, the Serbs retreated from behind the agreed lines, Sarajevo was united under the Muslim control. Bosnia and Herzegovina was destroyed as a Serbian country and divided into three entities, ruled by the Muslims. NATO was saved and brought a stone's throw away from Russia. In the military sense, Dayton was a complete success for the Americans.

I wasn't present in Dayton, but I got in touch with Holbrooke in 2006 and 2007. Then, I repeated to him the initiative for Radovan Karadzic and Ratko Mladic to surrender in Serbia and to be tried in Belgrade. I had the support of "Joan B. Kroc"

Institute for Peace and Justice, managed by the wife of the founder of *MacDonald's Company,* whose value was estimated at 50 billion dollars. This San Diego Institute allocated 30 million dollars for establishing a Department of the Hague Tribunal where Karadzic and Mladic would be tried.

The Institute for Peace and Justice insisted on including Richard Holbrooke in this new campaign, since he was a world-known politician who would give it the international legitimacy. I asked for the support and opinion of Richard Holbrooke on that. I suggested to Holbrooke, although he was just a lawyer at the time, that he should assist me in resolving the fate of Dr Radovan Karadzic. Holbrooke, who had signed an agreement on non-aggression with Karadzic, rejected this initiative of mine. Holbrooke was even then, as a US civilian, a fierce opponent of Radovan Karadzic and all other dangerous Serbs.

At the Peace Conference in Dayton, where there was no discussion on Serbia and the Kosovo issue, Richard Holbrooke, secretly, through his Albanian couriers, passed to Slobodan Milosevic a document that implied a wide autonomy for Kosovo and Metohija, but not the independence of the Southern Serbian Province. Nebojsa Vujovic wrote about this, in my opinion, greatest secret of Dayton, in his book *The Last Flight from Dayton. Closed Door Negotiations.*

"John Barley approached me and told me we needed to speak in private. He took out a document of approximately ten, fifteen pages, put it on the desk and said: 'Nebojsa, in the *Holiday Inn* Hotel, Bujar Bukoshi has been staying for some time now. He is an Albanian from Frankfurt and a representative of Ibrahim Rugova in Europe. With the organization of some friends of his from the USA, he brought (Ibrahim) Rugova here. Rugova is also in the *Holiday Inn.* We've had a meeting with them and we've made a draft document on the resolution of the Kosovo situation.'

I told him that that was a peace conference on Bosnia and Herzegovina and that Kosovo wasn't on the agenda and I demanded that he explained what that was about. He replied that their experts and diplomats had been having talks with the representatives of the Albanians from Kosovo for several months in order to somehow calm down the situation there, which was unbearable, and to ind a comprehensive political solution for Kosovo," Nebojsa Vujovic wrote.

The document on the desk envisaged the provision of a wide autonomy to Kosovo in order to make the Albanians satisfied, the creation of their institutions, which they had long abandoned, and ensuring them the possibility to organize their own life and development. The centralized influence from Belgrade was supposed to be reduced, but Barley claimed that the resolution implied Kosovo to remain within Serbia and that it didn't envisage the independence.

The attitude of the US administration, and particularly the group of congressmen who talked with President Clinton, was that the Peace Conference in Ohio should be used to expand the topic and ind the comprehensive solution for both Bosnia and Kosovo. That group of congressmen was led by Eliot Engel, New York Congressman, and Dana Rohrabacher, California Congressman. Prior to that, the two of them had co-sponsored at least 25 resolutions in the US Congress with various condemnations of Serbia due to the situation in Kosovo. In their opinion, Kosovo was the next potential crisis that was already knocking at Serbian door.

In 1995, when the complex issue of Bosnia and Herzegovina was being resolved, the Americans considered that Dayton was an opportunity to resolve everything in one go, including the relation between Serbia and Kosovo and Metohija Province.

According to Nebojsa Vujovic, Mr. Barley told him:

"Please, hand over this document, which is quite balanced and harmonized, to President Milosevic. Tell him that the US leadership and President Clinton have accepted to include this topic in the conference. Let the President Milosevic take a look at the draft of the Kosovo solution and the accompanying documents on the amendments to the Kosovo Constitution and the USA will perform the appropriate political and any other pressure on its disposal so that the Albanians from Kosovo accept this solution. They have already obtained the principal agreement of Ibrahim Rugova. He wants to talk with President Milosevic. The weekend is approaching, there will be fewer people in the base, and it will be a good opportunity for them to talk in secrecy."

When Vujovic handed this Albanian document to the President, Milosevic read it and stood up angrily. He then firmly crumpled the papers and threw them at the Vujovic's face.

"Are they fucking with me? Who do they take me for? What Kosovo? That's an internal issue of Serbia. It's out of the question! Tell your Washington friends that it's out of the question to fuck with me! 'cause, if they wanna fuck with me, they'll get some good fucking!"

Nebojsa Vujovic stated that he had returned the crumpled papers to Barley and that he had paraphrased Milosevic's assertion saying that the crisis in Bosnia and Herzegovina was being resolved in Dayton and that Kosovo was an internal issue of Serbia. Barley took the papers and said:

"Okay, Nebojsa. I'll inform the US delegation. I'll tell that to Richard Holbrooke and Christopher Hill. They'll notify the US leadership. Just, I think, Nebojsa, that, by this, you are maybe missing the last chance to resolve the Kosovo situation in a harmonized, balanced, generally accepted manner and that, probably, the trouble is yet to come."

I agree with Vujovic, who concluded that, owing to the rage and spite of Milosevic, we, the Serbs, missed an opportunity to rationally catch even a meager opportunity that the heritage of Kissinger's politics could have provided – the rational discussion of all sides and a politically realistic resolution of the issue. Even of the Kosovo and Metohija issue, which the Americans saved for their final clash with the belligerent Milosevic.

"Instead of peaceful negotiations, with this reaction of Milosevic, we again fell into the hands of the politics of Zbigniew Brzezinski – 'hit and rule'," said Nebojsa Vujovic.

That is exactly what happened. Three years later, the US diplomacy guru, Henry Kissinger, announced to Nebojsa Vujovic the American-Albanian war against Milosevic and Serbia:

"You missed your opportunity in Dayton. Now you'll get hit."

The letter of the President George W. Bush to Dr Borko Djordjevic

RUGOVA'S KOSOVO

Kosovo and Metohija is the heart of Serbia, the cradle of the Serbian people, the temple of Serbian faith and soul, the land of national identity. That is a territory that cannot be bought or taken away from Serbs. It was first conquered by Vukan, the Grand Prince of Serbia, in 1091, when he took Zvecan, and then by the Grand Prince Stefan Nemanja, who entered Lipljan in 1106. After the fall of Constantinople in 1204, Kosovo and Metohija became the center of the medieval Serbia. Apart from all these historical facts and findings, Albanian nationalists, with the help of various allies, have been trying to snatch Kosovo from us for a century and a half.

The Albanians, originating from the Byzantine area, settled in Serbia and the Balkans together with the Turks. Then, we called them Arbanas or Arnauts. They started politically organizing in 1878, when they established an association in Prizren named the League for Defending Albanian Rights, and, then, in 1918, the Committee for Defending Kosovo was created. That is how they started expressing their attitude on the political rights to living space and autonomy within Serbia. Their allies were Turks, Englishmen, Italians, and Germans. They organized their terrorist groups and troops of ballistae. We defeated them in the Balkan Wars, in the Great War, and in the Second World War. After the Balkan and the Great War, the settlement of Serbs to Kosmet was increased.

Josip Broz Tito, the creator of the second Yugoslavia, wishing to create the Balkan Federation, brought hundreds of thousands of Albanians from Albania to Kosmet. He gave them a national identity and offered Kosmet to Albania. Tito prohibited the return of the Serbs who were exiled from the province during the war, and thus favored Albanians. Broz not only prohibited the return of the colonists that King Aleksandar had settled in Kosovo and Metohija, but he approved the destruction of the Serbian property. The property was devastated, burned, or appropriated during the war, which was confirmed by the decision of the Committee for the Agrarian Reform and Colonization of the FNRY in 1946.

With the support of Serbian workers and communists, Josip Broz declared the Autonomous Region of Kosovo and Metohija in 1945, which he renamed into the Autonomous Province of Kosovo and Metohija in 1963. In November 1968, it was renamed into the Socialist Autonomous Province of Kosovo, omitting the name Metohija. Since then, it has been a federal unit of the SFRY and Serbia.

However, the divisions instigated by the communist authorities of Yugoslav orientation, while Serbian authorities remained silent, deepened the gap between the Serbian and the Albanian people in Kosmet. For instance, at the beginning of 1964, overnight, the Albanians raised Albanian lags throughout Kosovo and Metohija. The Albanians were the only national minority in Yugoslavia without a lag. They'd received a hint from Albania to protest and, since 1966, they have continuously been raising the flag of another country, Albania, as their own all over Serbia.

At the beginning of the 1970s, my friends from Belgrade told me that, in Pristina, there was one promenade for Serbs and the other for Albanians. The cinema projections were performed separately for the Serbs and the Albanians. There were Albanian taverns and Serbian taverns. The government did everything to separate the two nations, instead of joining them to live together.

Slobodan Milosevic and Ibrahim Rugova

In 1974, in Palm Springs, where I lived, I saw a banner saying: "The Republic of Kosovo!". It was placed by Albanian immigrants in the USA, and the US authorities didn't react to it. They considered it a democratic right of Albanian immigrants. In my opinion, Kosovo was back then in the hands of the Albanians, but it took us, the Serbs, twenty years to realize that. And, then, it was too late!

In the meantime, Fadil Hoxha, Adem Demaçi, and Ibrahim Rugova became the political leaders of Albanian nationalists in the 1970s and 1980s. They were supported by Albania, the USSR, China, Great Britain, Germany, and the USA. They organized insurgencies against the Serbian Government in 1968, at the beginning of the '70s, and at the beginning of the '80s, as well as at the beginning of 1990.

According to the data of a historian, Radoslav Ð. Gaćinovic, from 1981 to 1988, there were 3,748 Albanians performing enemy operations in Kosmet, 6,379 anti-Yugoslav fliers were distributed, and 14,725 slogans "Kosovo - Republic" were written. 1,220 persons were convicted of committing acts of political crime and 3,068 Shqiptars were punished for misdemeanor.

While Milosevic was a solid ally of the USA, in September 1991, the Albanians from Kosovo organized a referendum for seceding from the SFRY and the SR of Serbia. The Authorities in the SR of Serbia declared the referendum illegal, but they didn't obstruct it. After the voting, the independence of Kosmet was declared, but it wasn't recognized by any UN member state, except Albania.

Not until the forming of the guerilla terrorist KLA, did Albanian terrorists move into a war against Serbia in 1997, which they won two years later with the help of NATO forces and the USA. In 2008, the new leader of the so-called independent Kosovo became a war criminal, a murderer, and a mobster, Hashim Thaçi, nicknamed "The Snake".

Becoming the head of the League of Communists, and then the head of Serbia, Slobodan Milosevic attempted to dampen the Albanian separatist aspirations in the Southern Province, as well as the autonomous aspirations in the Northern Province, Vojvodina, by performing the centralization of the republic. It was the time without Tito, when Slovenian and Croatian leadership aroused the Albanian nationalism with their attacks at Serbia. In such atmosphere, Milosevic directly faced the Albanian demands for the independence of education.

Referring to the Constitution of the SFRY from 1977 that leaves the right to the republics and provinces to organize the school system, with possible mutual agreement, from 1989 Albanian teachers and professors worked according to the old province programs, and not in accordance with the new Serbian program. Parallel school systems, Serbian and Albanian, were created and the country tried to prohibit that. Albanian educationists responded with strikes and demonstrations. Since 1990, coursebooks and workbooks have been printed labeled with "the Republic of Kosovo". That Albanian school system, with 400,000 students and 20,000 teachers, was funded by the Albanian nationalist emigration. The curriculum of this educational system was changed "in accordance with the Constitution of Kaçanik" and it increasingly differed from the ones that Serbian students in Kosmet had. The Slavs were erased from history and the Illyrians, as the ancestors of the Albanian nation, were inserted. Milos Obilic was deleted and a new, invented Albanian hero was introduced – Misici.

Separatism was in full swing in 1993, to such an extent that there were even public considerations on the territorial division of Kosovo and Metohija within Serbia. The first President of the FRY, Dobrica Ćosic, agreed on the division of Kosovo and Metohija with the leader of Albanians, Ibrahim Rugova, in 1993, but Slobodan Milosevic prevented that.

The controversial point was that Dobrica believed that Slobodan Milosevic was supposed to withdraw from of ice of the President of Serbia and to give way to others from his party in order to get a greater opportunity to cooperate with foreign countries.

It turned out later that the USA and other countries had made clear arrangements with Milosevic and entered the agreements with him. Slobodan grew stronger with the US support.

In order to solve the problem of insurgency and seizing of the school system, Milosevic secretly negotiated with Ibrahim Rugova, the leader of the Democratic League of Kosovo and the first man of Kosovo Albanians at the time, for several weeks during 1995. The members of the humanitarian Community "Sant'Egidio" assisted them in those secret negotiations. That is a private Catholic community located in Rome.

Rugova was approximately the same age as Sloba. He was born in 1944 in Istok and he was a professor of literature by profession. As an Albanian of Yugoslav orientation, Rugova saw Kosovo as a Province with strong autonomy. The two of them reached an agreement and signed a document on the return of the students and educators of Albanian nationality into public schools. Then, at the beginning of 1996, Slobodan Milosevic and Ibrahim Rugova sat behind a negotiating table for the first time. Americans interpreted the signing of the document on the return of Albanian school staff into public schools of Serbia with their comment that it was "a precedent by which the Serbian government officially recognizes the legitimacy of the leading Albanian organization from Kosovo and its disputed leader Rugova".

With this move, Rugova defeated Milosevic. Rugova obtained political points at the ultra-Albanian plan, by which Albanian pupils and the separatist Albanian movement actually defeated the politics of Slobodan Milosevic in Kosovo and Metohija. The leaders of Kosovo Serbs and the leaders of Serbian opposition stated the same, because they said that Milosevic secretly negotiated with Rugova, "behind the back of the Serbian nation".

THE RAMBOUILLET FAILURE

In his public appearances abroad at the end of 1990s, the Albanian leader Rugova, who was adored by the USA and Germany, said on several occasions that the KLA didn't belong to the nation, and that he was fighting for the autonomy of Kosovo and not for the independent Kosovo. During his stay in Italy, in 1998, he publicly announced that Milosevic can be negotiated with in relation to the autonomy. During all the three official meetings with Milosevic, in 1998 and 1999, the peacemaker Ibrahim Rugova spoke about the autonomy of Kosmet. However, the firm and insolent Milosevic wouldn't allow him to. He didn't even want to hear about the autonomy of Kosovo and Metohija during the time when he was the Archon of all the Serbs in the world.

The USA supported Ibrahim Rugova and his peacekeeping politics. The extent to which Dr Ibrahim Rugova had become an American man was completely clear several years later when Congressman Joe DioGuardi, Senator Bob Dole, and Ambassador Warren Zimmermann came to visit him. They became Albanian lobbyists in the USA and the world. DioGuardi visited Kosovo for the second time in May 1990 and then several times again during the years that followed.

The firmness of the bond between Ibrahim Rugova and the USA is reflected in two facts. The first is that, at the request of the Albanians in Pristina, the American Information Center was formed, which our Government immediately denoted as another base of Washington and CIA in Kosovo and Metohija. The second occurred in the mid-1977 when Rugova intended to schedule a referendum for the Albanian Parliament, but the USA explicitly and publicly prohibited that. And, Ibrahim Rugova obeyed them, justifying that he would schedule them in the fall.

When the Americans realized that Ibrahim couldn't handle Sloba on his own, they sent Richard Holbrooke to assist him. President Bill Clinton was convinced that Holbrooke would break Milosevic and persuade him to listen to Rugova.

Holbrooke met Milosevic for the last time in January 1999. He offered Sloba a document named the *Interim Agreement for Peace and Self-Government in Kosovo* as the last chance to accept the agreement with Ibrahim Rugova on the autonomy of Kosmet within Serbia and to confirm it at the Rambouillet Peace Conference on 6th February 1999.

"Kosovo would regain its autonomy, the KLA would be disarmed, and the peace forces and NATO would be deployed on the regions where the Albanian terrorists are operating, Serbia remains whole," Holbrooke said to the Serbian Archon.

The representatives of the government in Serbia and Kosovo Albanians participated in the conference in the French Castle Rambouillet, near Paris, with the mediation of the envoys from the USA, Russia, and the EU: Christopher Hill, Boris Majorski, and Wolfgang Petritsch. The Albanian delegation included: Azem Sulja, Bajram Kosumi, Blerim Shala, Bujar Bukoshi, Edita Tahiri, Fehmi Agani, Hashim Thaçi, Hidajet Hiseni, Ibrahim Rugova, Idriz Ajeti, Jakup Krasniqi, Mehmet Hajrizi, Ramë Buja, Rexhep Qosja, Veton Surroi, and Xhavit Haliti.

The Serbian delegation was led by Ratko Marovic, and it also included: Vladan Kutlesic, Nikola Sainovic, Vladimir Stambuk, Vojislav Zivkovic, Guljbehar Sabovic, Zejnelabedin Kurejsi, Faik Jashari, Sokolj Ćuse, Re ik Sinadinovic, Ibro Vait, Ljuan Koka, and Ćerim Abazi.

The Albanian delegation at the Rambouillet Conference

The delegation of Kosovo Albanians, which was, to everyone's surprise, but with the great support of the USA, led by the then little-known Head of Guerillas Hashim Thaçi, accepted in principle the draft of the agreement for the resolution of the Kosovo crisis. Slobodan Milosevic rejected the peace plan and agreement, probably convinced that he could defeat Albanians and Americans. He wasn't satisfied with the proposals of holding the referendum in Kosovo on the autonomy and independence after three years, as well as of NATO taking control of the entire Serbian region. NATO guaranteed the sovereignty and territorial integrity of the FRY, but Milosevic didn't want to accept that either, understanding these proposals as an attack on his government and rule.

The members of the Serbian delegation in Rambouillet, prone to conspiracy theories, were convinced that the peace agreement on Kosmet was nothing but a gambling attempt of Madeleine Albright and Holbrooke's "bulldozer" diplomacy to wrest Kosovo from Serbia using skillful manipulation. And, in case that didn't work, to find an official pretext for a war against Serbia.

Annex B, which was dictated by the Americans several hours before the end of the negotiations, practically meant, according to them, the NATO occupation of the entire territory of the FR of Yugoslavia. Milosevic's men didn't consider the idea that the third Yugoslavia could join NATO and, thus, avoid "the occupation".

The failure of the Rambouillet conference, after seventeen days of unsuccessful negotiations, signified the end of the attempts to resolve the Kosovo crisis in a peaceful manner. The warning of the Russians, conveyed by Milan Komnenic, that the USA and NATO would punish him by bombarding the FRY, didn't make Milosevic change his attitude.

"The belief of Milosevic that the bombs won't be dropped is a big delusion. We cannot prevent that," Russians said.

Hearing that, the Archon Milosevic arrogantly replied to Komnenic: "You're just a scaremonger like your Vuk Draskovic. Holbrooke is coming, everything's going to be all right..."

That is how Slobodan Milosevic turned his private war with the Americans and NATO, which he considered would enslave Serbia upon its entrance, into the severe calamity of his own nation and other citizens of Serbia. Milosevic wasn't wise enough to prevent the worst from happening. He could have solved the Kosmet issue without a war. The same as Tito enrolled the second Yugoslavia into NATO, Milosevic could have become a member of the Western military alliance with the third Yugoslavia. That was exactly what my school friend Milan Milutinovic suggested to Madeleine Albright. At a meeting before the Rambouillet, when Milutinovic told her that Serbia was ready to join NATO, Ms. Albright indirectly told him that it was too late:

"No, that's not our option now."

It would have been much smarter if we had joined NATO than to be bombarded by them. That would provide us, the Serbs, peace and better future.

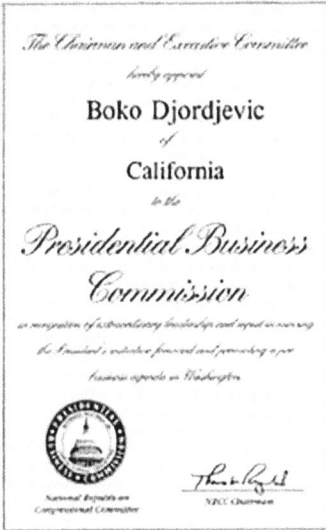

US President George W. Bush invites Dr. Borko Djordjevic from California to Washington

NATO IN SERBIA

Upon that, as retaliation against Milosevic, NATO was dropping uranium bombs on the entire nation for 78 days. By signing the Kumanovo Peace Agreement, Milosevic handed Kosmet to the Albanian nationalists. At that point, Milosevic was afraid that NATO would level the FRY to the ground and that it would occupy it with its land forces. He agreed to everything. The Resolution 1244 was adopted in the UN Security Council. The Kumanovo Agreement was signed by a General of the Yugoslav Army Svetozar Marjanovic, a Police General Obrad Stevanovic, and a British General Michael Jackson. This document envisaged the cessation of hostilities between the NATO forces and the forces of the Yugoslav Army and the Serbian police, as well as the withdrawal of the army and police from the region of Kosovo and Metohija within eleven days.

The withdrawal of Serbian forces occurred, as well as the establishment of the interim administrative management of the UN over the Southern Serbian province. The Americans and NATO entered the FRY. The military base Bondsteel was set up. The safety zone from the administrative border with Kosovo and Metohija inside the territory of Yugoslavia was defined and it was five kilometers on the ground and twentyfive kilometers in the air. The KFOR undertook the obligation to disarm the KLA. Then, the tendency of the Americans was realized in practice, best expressed by Christopher Hill that "there should be nothing green in Kosovo, and even if there was, it should be painted blue", having in mind, of course, the UN uniforms.

Milosevic brought the NATO bombers to Serbia

The entire Rambouillet scenario was, thus, conducted by force and realized during the following decades in its worst aspect for the Serbs.

Then, the USA decided to exclude Ibrahim Rugova from the process of the Pristina and Belgrade dialogue. He was the representative of moderate and, at the time, majority of Albanians, who weren't supporters of the armed insurrection and terrorist actions. At his place, the Americans installed the terrorists and mobsters, Hashim Thaçi and Ramush Haradinaj.

Instead of liquidating these two terrorists, Milosevic made a mistake and raised the entire Serbian army against the Albanian nationalists and the Albanian people. That is how Sloba made the ordinary Albanians, the FRY citizens, enemies of Serbia and the Serbs. Milosevic also betrayed the Serbs in Kosmet, who he had promised, back in 1986, that no one was allowed to beat them. But, they could bombard them, which was exactly what NATO did in 1999. Slobodan Milosevic destroyed the Serbian Kosovo. The uranium bombs still "kill" both the Serbs and the Albanians in Kosmet, because they die of cancer.

Drago Kovacevic, the last Serbian Mayor of Knin, who lived through the rule of Slobodan Milosevic in Croatia and Serbia, claims today that the surrender of Kosmet to the Albanians was the consequence of Milosevic's politics of deceit of the Serbian people and his trade with Serbian nation on account of Tuđman and Thaçi:

"The breakup of the SFRY started with Kosmet, went through the fate of the Republic of Srpska and two Serbian Krajinas in Croatia, in order to end in losing Kosovo and Metohija. The war in the SFRY opened because of the division of Bosnia and Herzegovina between Milosevic and Tuđman. It finished with Kosovo, because of the war between Milosevic and the Americans. First, he betrayed the Americans and, then they punished him. But they also punished the Serbian people. That betrayal wasn't so obvious, because the Americans always masked it with negotiations, agreements, discussions between, for instance, Milosevic and Rugova. Milosevic and Rugova then met again in front of the judges and guards of the Hague Tribunal, on 3rd May 2002. Rugova was an Albanian peace-maker in Gandhi-like manner and with the Communist past. Milosevic protected him from Albanian nationalists, because he needed him as 'a good Albanian he can talk to.'"

With such a status, Ibrahim Rugova had a physical protection of the Serbian Secret Police, which led him to talks with Sloba, and with Milan Milutinovic as well, in Belgrade, Skopje, and Rome. The Serbian Secret Service brought Rugova to Belgrade in March 1999. When he was led to Slobodan Milosevic, the Archon persuaded him that the two of them should sign a joint press release on how they had reached the "absolute concurrence and that they are jointly choosing a political process and peaceful resolution of the Kosovo crisis". Rugova says he was forced to do that.

Then, Rugova was brought again in May 1999, just to be transferred to Rome, because the KLA threatened to kill him and held him in house arrest in Pristina. With Milosevic's mediation, even the ruler of Libya, Colonel Muammar Al Gadda i was preparing to welcome Ibrahim Rugova in Tripoli, but as the Serbs had transferred him to Rome, Colonel Gadda i, feeling tricked, ceased all diplomatic relations with Belgrade.

Owing to his attitude on autonomy, Rugova was exposed to political pressures and death threats by the KLA members and Albanian nationalists from Pristina and Tirana. Milosevic had to provide him protection or Albanians would kill him. However, those pressures were fruitful, since Rugova changed his attitude and, from Rome, told the media:

"The Serbs are no longer entitled to Kosovo. The confederation of Kosovo with Albania is the question of the future."

From that point, Rugova became the favorite of Bill Clinton. Meanwhile, NATO was bombarding Serbia and Kosmet. Ibrahim Rugova became the democratically elected and internationally recognized President of Kosovo, while Milosevic was losing elections, his presidential position and freedom, and finally got into the custody of the Hague Tribunal.

Persuaded by Bill Clinton, Rugova went to the Hague Tribunal where he appeared, in 2002, as a protected witness at the trial of Slobodan Milosevic. Ibrahim Rugova arrived before the Hague Tribunal more like a rather vulnerable witness of the prosecution, than as a trump card that Carla del Ponte's team of prosecutors could actually earn much points from. Milosevic assisted him to leave the courtroom untainted and, upon his return to Pristina as the President of Kosovo, to get rows of people waiting for him considering that he had convincingly testified on the calamities of his Albanian nation.

The two of them died approximately at the same time, in 2006 -Sloba as a prisoner in the Hague prison, and Ibrahim as a free citizen inside his home in Pristina.

HOW TO ASSASSINATE THE PRESIDENT

The political destiny of Slobodan Milosevic was determined precisely in Kosovo and Metohija, when he said to the Serbs gathered in Kosovo Polje: "No one is allowed to beat you!" The fact that Milosevic was bonded to the Serbs from Kosovo, was used by the USA and the CIA to do away with the Serbian Archon precisely through the development of the events in this province.

The first attempt to assassinate Milosevic was conducted in 1989 during the celebration of 600 years since the Kosovo Battle in Gazimestan. It had been planned for Slobodan Milosevic to arrive in Kosovo Polje from Pristina by car. As there had been heavy rainfall the night before the gathering, the fields of Kosmet were wet and hundreds of cars and buses got stuck in the dense and black mud. Therefore, Dragan Mitrovic, the Head of the State Security Service of Serbia (SDB) at the time, decided to transport Milosevic by helicopter of the Serbian police. The President of Serbia came by car from Belgrade to Krusevac and, from there, by helicopter directly to Kosovo Polje. The field control from Krusevac to Gracanica showed that the State Security Service was right when they had indicated to the President the danger of travelling to Gazimestan. Near Podujevo, the SDB inspectors found an automatic sniper rifle, and, according to the evidence, it could be concluded that it belonged to a Shqiptar assassinator of Slobodan Milosevic.

Gazimestan, the place of the glory and death of Slobodan Milosevic

That information that Shqiptars were preparing the assassination of the President of Serbia was obtained from the Russian KGB. That was why Slobodan Milosevic, in Gazimestan, on Vidovdan in 1989, had the strongest possible personal security. Immediately after his speech, Slobodan Milosevic returned home the same way he had arrived, via Krusevac. The members of the SFRY Presidency returned by small airplanes of the Federation, accompanied by the federal police and the YNA security.

Then, when the USA and the CIA announced the personal war against Slobodan Milosevic, placed him on the most-wanted list, and offered 5 million dollars for his head, various spies and assassinators were waiting for their opportunity all around Serbia to kill Slobodan. However, until June 2000, no one in Yugoslavia succeeded in earning 5 million dollars, the amount the USA offered for the head of President Slobodan Milosevic. The Serbian Archon was still on the throne. A protest of malcontents at the opposition rally in Belgrade, on 14th April 2000, and the fact that 65% of the citizens of Serbia wanted Milosevic's resignation were not sufficient to overthrow the President of Yugoslavia. Some external influence was needed in order to turn the internal rebellion against Milosevic into his final downfall.

The opposition leaders sought support to finally confront Slobodan Milosevic both from Moscow and Washington. Until 1995, Slobodan Milosevic was a rather useful US partner. After all, he did sign the Dayton Agreement in the middle of the USA, with the intention to obtain peace and introduce the international military and political control of Bosnia and Herzegovina. In the Rambouillet Agreement, Milosevic left some space to the USA to intervene in Kosmet, which they used through NATO in March 2000. That didn't undermine the political integrity of this Serbian leader in any way. On the contrary, meanwhile, Slobodan Milosevic, a son of a priest from Pozarevac, as a former President of Serbia, was appointed the first man of the third Yugoslavia in the summer of 1997.

As his biographers wrote, in 1997, Slobodan Milosevic achieved what his wife Dr Mira Markovic had predicted to him while he was still in the army in Zadar – he became the second Tito! Milosevic lived and worked at the addresses that related him to Josip Broz – in Uzicka Street and in the White Palace (Beli Dvor). Just, this time, Pozarevac was proclaimed the Serbian Kumrovec.

At the end of the millennium and at the beginning of the 21st century, the USA suddenly started a serious hunt after the Serbian Archon. First, Madeleine Albright forced the Hague indictment against the first man of Serbia, and then, NATO sought him with its missiles. An American bomb was dropped on Milosevic's residence in Dedinje. The guardians of his name and work declared that it was a US assassination attempt of a president of a sovereign country. Later, the US and NATO bombers' missiles sought the President of the FRY in his war shelter in Dobanovci, but as Serbian people would jokingly say – the President Milosevic wasn't at work at the time.

In the opinion of the Colonel Dragan Vuksic, the war against the FRY was actually retaliation against Slobodan Milosevic.

"There was no war in the FRY, but a clash of two authoritarian wills: the will of Slobodan Milosevic that subjected his country to incredible calamities and the will of NATO that was ready to destroy and kill. The Yugoslav Army in Kosovo was abused as never before. It was fighting an already lost battle just to be withdrawn from Kosmet by the same regime, without any remorse, under the terms dictated by NATO, leaving Serbian, Montenegrin, and other non-Albanian nations to the mercy of Albanian terrorists and NATO. That wasn't a war. It was a punishment of a nation, a well-weighed retaliation for wrong politics," considers Dragan Vuksic, a former Colonel of the Yugoslav Army, who was retired at his own request in September 1999, due to his disagreement with the politics and behavior of the state and military authorities.

Putting Slobodan Milosevic and the members of his family and party on the lists of persons forbidden from entering Europe and the USA during 1999, narrowed the movement of the President and his closest associates. When the USA, in the fall of 1999, offered five million dollars to Serbian head hunters for catching Slobodan Milosevic, dead or alive, no one in Serbia dared turn this opportunity into a chance to get rich.

As all threats of the CIA, and particularly the attack of NATO and the USA against Yugoslavia, as well as the loss of Kosmet, didn't contribute to overthrowing Milosevic, Yugoslav and Balkan public started wondering about the secret of Milosevic's survival. One of the theses put in the circulation was that Slobodan Milosevic was actually an American man and that everything he was doing was in the interest of the USA and Washington. Thus, in return, the USA was supporting him in the morning and overthrowing him a bit, in the afternoon. This thesis was publicly expressed by Milan Gorjanc, a Colonel of the Slovenian Army and one of the best military experts in Slovenia, the former Director of the Center for Strategic Studies, at the beginning of March 2000 in a Montenegrin magazine *Monitor*. He simply wondered how it was possible that, during the ten years of his rule, Slobodan Milosevic destroyed the SFRY, broke and submitted Serbian lands, made Serbs lee, lost Kosmet, embarrassed Serbia, and, remained the head of Yugoslavia, nevertheless.

Even when the war with NATO was lost, because Kosmet went into the hands of Shqiptars, and later colonized by Americans and Germans, Slobodan Milosevic was still just strengthening his power in Yugoslavia, or, to be more precise, in Serbia.

A columnist Aleksandar Tijanic elaborated on the topic whether Milosevic was an American man or a spy and, because of that, constantly on power. The Americans, according to Tijanic, first made Milosevic into "the globally best recognized enemy of the USA, gave him the title of the leader of the rest of the world against the dollar and the new world order and gravity, thereby contributing to the hormonal disorder of the Serbian regime, which imagined that it had grown to that extent that the future of the entire galaxy would be drawn in Belgrade".

Accused of war crimes during the bombardment, flooded with requests, of even Patriarch Pavle, to resign, Milosevic found his salvation in the Americans. His remuneration was the statement of Madeleine Albright that he would resign from power at the regular democratic elections. That was the hint to the leaders of the opposition that they could ask for nothing more than for the official request, even if it was at rallies, to schedule elections at all levels.

According to the viewpoints of many Americans, but also of Europeans and Russians, and finally of Serbian analysts, the war of NATO against the FRY was actually the greatest warning and threat to Slobodan Milosevic. With that attack, the USA wanted to stir the internal fire of rebellion of the Serbs against their Archon. The Serbs remained silent and swallowed the defeat from the USA and Albania.

However, losing Kosovo didn't overthrow Milosevic, which is still a phenomenon that can hardly be explained.

The second thesis which justified that defeat was that the war against the FRY was a battle against the Serbs, against a powerful military force in the Balkans and the Russian outpost in the South of Europe.

After that, many other American and European threats ensued; from the one that the FRY would be divided and turned into a new Cuba, to the one that the CIA would cause a civil war between the Serbs and the Montenegrins. As the sword of Damocles above Milosevic's head, the Americans placed the Montenegrin ultimatum on remaining in the federation of the FRY. They paid Montenegrins for that in many green dollars.

It is undeniable that sanctions, the persecution of the Serbian people, and the bombardment just consolidated Milosevic on his throne, instead of overthrowing him. It is unclear how the Americans and the Europeans couldn't see and realize that. Some of them did, but the USA always remained true to its politics that if you draw a pistol, you must shoot from it. Shooting at Milosevic, however, they also hit the Serbian people and their country.

Milosevic ruled over politics, legislation, finances, media, diplomacy, army, police, unions, health, and education, but he was powerless in the face of reality, in the face of life.

The world clash with Slobodan Milosevic was an American and European fight with Communism in the Balkans. The hunt after Milosevic was a process that continued inside, in Yugoslavia, and outside, in the Western world, and which would be finalized the moment the last traces of Communism died in the FRY. Until that point, the West, and particularly the USA, continued to support him in the morning and overthrow him in the afternoon, because the Serbian Archon was the president that could give them most.

"The West still doesn't want Slobodan Milosevic removed from the power."

That was a statement of Scott Taylor, a publisher and the editor of a Canadian military magazine *Esprit de Corps* and the author of the book *Inat.*

The scenario of overthrowing Sloba was activated during January 2000 in Moscow, where Boris Yeltsin was retired overnight, and the KGB Colonel Vladimir Putin became the new President of Russia. Putin didn't want to cooperate with Milosevic, but he wanted to cooperate with his wife, Mira Markovic. At the same time, Bill Clinton signed a plan of the intelligence operation of the blockade of Slobodan Milosevic, filed under the code *Matrix.* According to that plan, the USA decided not to hunt and overthrow President Milosevic with the US army in Serbia. Instead, the Americans left the issue of the survival of Slobodan Milosevic and his regime to be resolved by the Serbian people, with some American assistance. That is how the 5th October occurred and Slobodan Milosevic was removed from power.

POISONED PEOPLE

I have quite often faced the question, which I was also wondering about – why did Serbian people support Slobodan Milosevic for that long, from 1986 to 2000?

Milosevic was an autocrat, a selfish and insolent man, a politically and socially illiterate ruler, and a cruel leader of the tormented Serbian people. The Americans supported him as an Archon although Milosevic didn't meet their political expectations – to create a new democratic Yugoslavia and, within it, a new free Serbia.

He originated from a poor Montenegrin family and educated in Yugoslavia and the USA. He felt the US democracy and capitalism and, there, he learned to rule with the state and market laws. He wasn't a diplomat, a man of compromises, intelligence, and wisdom. He didn't balance to keep Serbia floating, but we all sank with him.

When he came to power in Serbia, he turned into an autocrat, a usurper of the state, public, and national property and into a rich man. He robbed Serbia together with his family members and destroyed it. In my opinion, for the destruction of Serbia and the Province of Kosovo, no one is to blame but Slobodan Milosevic. His politics consisted of expressing what he didn't want and not what he wanted.

Dana Popovic, a Professor at the Faculty of Economics, saw from her personal experience that Slobodan Milosevic had awoken the worst face of Serbia:

"Of all the bad faces of Serbia, Milosevic awoke the worst one with his rule. He raised insolent and incompetent people to the sky limits for personal power. He assassinated journalists. He created and brought up almost all current tycoons. And, what is worse than that, because it can always be worse: his Serbia is the country of Badza, Bidza, and Bulidza, of bandits, brutes, and bullies. And, of State Security Administration (UDBA). And, he even turned the UDBA into a commercial organization. We could learn about our future from *Duga*, from the texts of Milosevic's wife."

Why did people let him do that?

My answer is quite simple – because Milosevic pampered Serbian people, he deceived, sacrificed, and destroyed them. Serbs love being deceived, sacrificed, and destroyed. That is Serbian personal trait, which matured through the centuries of misfortune that had struck them. The Serbs love to be hurt, and, then, to suffer and grieve, to spend centuries retelling the legends on their lost battles and killed heroes. That's the spiritual food of this nation, their sustenance. The Serbs love living in the past, in the stories that never end, because they are afraid of the reality and they are most afraid of being responsible for the reality.

The historical truth is that Serbia is a political and traffic crossroads of three continents, a "roadhouse", as Jovan Cvijic called it, destroyed by many armies. That thesis was constantly modified by Milosevic and adapted to his own political conspiracy theories.

When proving the relevance of a question the international community would pose, Slobodan Milosevic would many times reach for his favorite conspiracy theory. He claimed that crimes against the Serbs, which, according to him, had been conducted ever since the distant past, not only in Kosmet, but in Croatia and Bosnia and Herzegovina as well, were "a direct consequence of anti-Serbian politics executed throughout the history with the intention to annul and alter the consequences of the First and Second World War." The main advocates of such politics, according to Milosevic, were unidentified German politicians who, at the beginning of 1990s resurrected the idea of abolishing Yugoslavia as a country which was created by the Versailles Treaty, after the First World War.

On the other hand, the support Germany gave to Ibrahim Rugova and the requests of Kosovo Albanians, according to Milosevic's claims, represented a kind of reward or debt repayment for "the great participation of Albanian formations on the side of Hitler and Mussolini in the Second World War".

The truth is, however, that we, as a nation, are guilty for all our calamities. Our rulers, from Aleksandar KaraDjordjevic to Slobodan Milosevic, didn't lead peaceful internal politics, but the one of war and haiduks. Genetically and politically, we are predetermined to be losers, and not winners. We behave like haiduks. We don't respect rules, agreements, and laws. We destroy everything we make, we work to our detriment just to prove the strength of our spite.

Milosevic, for instance, was killing his Serbian people in several different ways. Black marketeers sold to people: oil and petrol mixed with water, smuggled cigarettes, which damaged their health, fake alcoholic drinks, stolen in Croatian and Bosnian factories, but added methyl, because of which several dozens of people died, smuggled drugs, which killed the drug addicts, and, in that way, made Serbia into a secret market of illegal narcotics with approximately 200,000 users. The Serbs accepted that, because they understood the criminalized life as their sacrificing for their homeland, as their fight against the enemy, but the truth is that the Serbs like to suffer, to be tortured and oppressed, to go through an ordeal and moan about it later. In addition, Serbian lives were very cheap. People were rapidly dying, of poverty and the poisons they consumed. And, no one complained because they thought it was patriotic sacrificing.

We, the Serbs, are incapable of real life. That's the root of Serbia's downfall – in the essence of incapable and ignorant people who aren't aware that their ignorance leads to downfall. The new millennium requires extensive knowledge, the investment of intellect and capital in the fight for the survival in the open market. Instead of that, we are returning to the past, constantly reviving the Serbian stories on the enemies of the nation. With those stories, Milosevic poisoned Serbian people. Telling stories about the past and conspiracies against Serbs, the Archon Milosevic was building and strengthening his power among people. Even today, many Serbian institutions, officials, statesmen, and functionaries, political parties and their presidents live from the legends and from the past.

Unfortunately, that is how the country, the church, and the crown have behaved for decades. Milosevic, as a ruler, fought for the preservation of the past, in which Serbs and Yugoslavs were comfortable. He cultivated self-government and communism. Milosevic fought to preserve the socialist self-government in the third Yugoslavia, because factory workers and directors were his voters. Serbian and Yugoslav companies funded his victories at the elections and his rise in politics.

For years, Milosevic nurtured the system in which, during work committees, even an illiterate cleaning lady could choose the director of her company, institution, or bank. At the end of the 20th and at the turn of the 21st century, Slobodan Milosevic nurtured the system that had already died in the neighboring republics and countries. Serbia and Montenegro, under his rule, lived in the past, and Slovenia lived in the future.

He hoped the YNA would save Yugoslavia and himself. That Yugoslav Army was enormous and strong, but inefficient. Its Serbian officers were rather Yugoslavs, Croatian and Slovenian sons-in-law than Serbian patriots. Their families were broken apart. Then, the YNA destroyed itself first, and, then, the country of the SFRY.

Milosevic didn't want the confederation with Yugoslavian republics in which each republic would be independent. He rejected the plan of Lord Carrington, offered at the meeting with the SFRY Presidency in 1991 in Tito's Villa in Igalo. Everyone accepted it, but Milosevic was the only to refuse the plan on confederation.

He didn't understand the world changes. That is how his heir Ivica Dacic explains this wrong politics of Milosevic.

Slobodan Milosevic understood the world changes quite well and it is precisely the reason why he was fighting for the past, so that the changes wouldn't occur and that he wouldn't get replaced. He fought for the failed Yugoslavia, no matter how incomplete, just for himself. It was important for him that Serbia would become a legal and political successor of the SFRY so that he could get its heritage – state property, billions of dollars, and Yugoslav gold in foreign banks. Just the League of Communists of Yugoslavia had been keeping as much as 45 billion dollars of the party membership fee in foreign banks ever since 1932.

Slobodan Milosevic behaved like a rowdy. And, it is a well-known fact that the Serbs prefer a rowdy to a hard worker or a professor. The typical example of that is the behavior of Slobodan Milosevic, who pretended to be a great archon. When, in the early '90s the directors of Beko Factory offered him a gift of a couple of elegant men suits, Milosevic rejected that present, saying:

"Thank you, my comrades, I can't take that gift, I'll buy myself a suit." He left the impression of a modest leader of the people and the country, who didn't want any privileges. Meanwhile, Milosevic was robbing the same people and the country, seizing billions of marks and taking them outside the country, and leading Serbia into misery.

Julian Harston, a former Assistant Secretary-General in the United Nations, once honestly said:

"Slobodan Milosevic was an amoral man!"

When Slobodan Milosevic arrived at the political scene, Yugoslavia was united and appreciated. When he left, Yugoslavia was torn apart, its economy was destroyed, and the world public perceived Serbs as villains. Milosevic first based his politics on the extreme nationalism. That is how he came to power. Then, he didn't attempt to protect the Serbs outside Serbia in any other way, except by using force. He sent paramilitary formations in Bosnia and Croatia to ethnically cleanse them.

It is ironic that Slobodan Milosevic destroyed almost everything he pretended he was protecting: both the former SFRY and the Serbian nation. In the meantime, Milosevic left the Serbs from Croatia and Bosnia to their evil fate, because it suited him so. Milosevic exiled the Serbs from Croatia, Bosnia and Herzegovina, Slovenia, and Macedonia, and pushed them in Serbia. He wasn't a nationalist, he just used the nationalism for his political purposes and, thereby, inflicted enormous defeats and embarrassments to the Serbian people.

Milosevic made for himself a new quasi-state, the FRY, and then the State Union of Serbia and Montenegro, in order to seize everything that had been Yugoslav. When Milosevic did that, Slovenia and Croatia started taking their share of the SFRY property, because there, as well, former communists came to power, representing themselves as democrats.

Dr Borko Djordjevic and the Crown Prince Aleksandar Karadjordjevic

LIVING IN THE PAST

The same as Milosevic, in the tumultuous 1990s, the Serbian Orthodox Church offered the past to people, and not the future. The church detached the Serbian people from the real life and kept them in the virtual religious world, where the main heroes were the saints: Saint Sava and Saint Nicholas. Although they mostly visit churches just at Christmas or Easter, the Serbs prefer listening to Church stories on the Kosovo battle, the Prince Marko, Milos Obilic, Saint George slaying the dragon, as well as on the hero Rasa, Radovan Karadzic, or General Ratko Mladic, to working on the economic or social development of Serbia and creating better future.

The case of the Pope not coming to Serbia depicts best how the Church, and the religious people with it, are the prisoners of the past. The Vatican and the Head of the Roman Catholic Church didn't recognize the so-called independent Kosovo and they took the side of Serbia. After his predecessor visited Banja Luka and Bosnian Serbs, the Pope Francis was ready to honor Serbia and visit Belgrade. The Serbian Orthodox Church didn't allow that, because the clergy believed that, with the arrival of Pope Francis, our church would lose its power among the Serbian people.

The Serbian Orthodox Church justified that act by saying that the Vatican hadn't condemned the crimes of the Catholics and Ustashas against the Serbs in Jasenovac during the Second World War. The Holy See was working on that, but they expected a direct cooperation with Serbia and our church, in return. The Serbian Orthodox Church and Patriarch Irinej refused that cooperation. The Serbian Patriarch didn't see that, by sending its Head to Serbia, the Vatican would improve the Serbian reputation in the Catholic world and rehabilitate Serbia after two decades of international attacks and criticisms. And, Serbia needed that to return to the international scene and to have our people regain their dignity. The Serbian Orthodox Church actually doesn't want to let Serbia be a dignified Christian country in the world.

The members of the KaraDjordjevic family, as the representatives of the crown, who returned to Serbia from their emigration in the

1990s, and then in 2001 permanently settled in the Royal Palace in Dedinje, are also the symbols of some past times, of the suffering inflicted to the royal family by communists. The KaraDjordjevic family is vegetating now, existing only on paper, and living from donations, and not from the fruits of their work. My neighbor, Prince Andrija, lived like a zombie in a tiny house in Palm Springs and waited for people to give him something because his father had been a king. He committed suicide because he couldn't continue living like that.

I have the impression that our people suffer from multiple personality disorder, because our people are at the same time Sloba, and Radovan, and Marko Kraljevic, and Saint Sava, but also Vladimir Putin, and they are the least of all – themselves, what their own name and surname represents. All this is happening because our people, insufficiently educated and aware, prefer legends, myths, and national reveries to the pure reality. All in all, one friend of mine defined the Serbian people like this: Serbs are a small, semi-literal nation, who has been deceived by someone to believe that they are a heavenly nation. The one who deceived the Serbian people was Slobodan Milosevic.

The Serbian national self has created a nation of losers, due to historical circumstances, non-functionality of the country, the church, and the crown, as well as due to the emotional character of the people. Unlike us, the Serbs, immersed in our emotions, hating rather than understanding other nations and religions, and making Catholics into our enemies, the Russians are brave, decisive, efficient, and true winners.

The Serbs invent enemies to themselves: the NATO, the USA, England, Croatians, Muslims, Montenegrins, Macedonians. They accuse Germans of aspiring to take the Vojvodina Province from us, thus, spreading fear among people, and then they moan about the misfortune that will strike us. Instead of having dialogues and making friendships, Serbs would rather threaten, clamor, confront, and then get killed.

The Serbian nation is diminishing and vanishing. The number of Serbian children being born is decreasing and the number of young people leaving Serbia is increasing. The country doesn't pay enough attention to the successful children and young people in the state or abroad. Novak Đokovic is today the best Serb in the world, but at home, in Belgrade, the government won't let him work. They take his sports fields and make threats. At the same time, municipal authorities do not even touch the owners of illegally constructed buildings, businessmen who deal with illegal trade and gray economy, or the people working in illegal health institutions.

For decades, Serbs, as losers, accused, for instance, Croatians and Catholics, for their failure and, thereby, empowered and strengthened Croatian nationalists, who, in the end, created a modern country –Croatia, which became a member of the EU. And, where is Serbia? Serbia is a prisoner of its history, its past, used for building the political authority by Slobodan Milosevic and Mira Markovic, then SPS and JUL, and finally by the Serbian country.

Unfortunately, Serbia is still facing with the legacy of Milosevic, even though it's been eighteen years since 5th October and twelve years since his death, because the damage he inflicted to our country with his politics is far from being fixed. In every problem arising nowadays, whether it is the loose economy, the destroyed infrastructure, the relations in the region, the relations with the USA and the EU, the world image of the Serbs, or the Kosovo issue, there is a bit of Milosevic in it, which indicates the depth of the scars he left behind.

We, the Serbs, always destroy ourselves, because we have the urge to destruct and then to be reborn from the ashes. Such behavior is the consequence of the historical traumas the Serbian nation has lived with. Always enslaved, occupied, fighting for survival, the people live with the traumas caused by the great calamities, the same as, for instance, a young woman raped as a child does.

Serbs are masochistic people, cruel to themselves, persecuting successful Serbs, and being kind to foreigners. We are modern *haiduks*, always violent, breaking our own laws, always dishonest to ourselves and our country. We are also modern Janissaries because we appreciate foreigners more than our brothers. We destroy ourselves and bow to the others. Milosevic listened to and respected the Americans more than his own Serbian political partners. Slobodan was actually afraid of the Americans.

Generally, we, the Serbs, are afraid of everyone and trust no one, not even ourselves. We cannot handle the fateful social and political problems. We are afraid of reality, so we escape into the world of dreams, of legends and lies, of conspiracy theories, and into the mystical history. The Serbs avoid the real world in order to live in the imaginary world of legends. That is why the Serbs talk about the history a lot, but work very little.

As a nation, the Serbs are enchanted with Americans, but 95% of us don't understand the American way of life or the US politics. Americans are realistic people faced towards the future, which they carefully plan. In the USA, the whole life is devoted to reality and future. People fight to live better from the day they were born till the inheritance. My daughter, Aleksandra, is supposed to inherit 40 million dollars from her American grandmother. Aleksandra Djordjevic doesn't mope about the sad fate of her grandmother, she is getting ready for the future, for her life with that wealth.

The Americans understand the Serbs and they support us, push us towards future. We, the Serbs, do not know what is waiting for us in the future, so we live one day at the time. We live from the tales of Serbian defeats and sufferings, as well as from the stories that things will get better one day.

THE DEMOCRATIC DESTRUCTION

When, two centuries ago, Milos Obrenovic, the Prince of Serbia, ordered the assassination of the Leader of Serbia, Karađorđe, he sent his head to Istanbul. From there, from the Ottoman Empire, the Prince received a hatt-i sharif in 1817 stating that he could be the ruler of the independent Principality of Serbia. When DOS arrested Slobodan Milosevic and extradited him to the Americans and the Hague Tribunal in 2001, President Vojislav Kostunica and the Prime Minister Zoran Đinđic received an approval to rule the democratic Serbia and the third Yugoslavia.

Milan St. Protic, a former Ambassador of the FRY in the USA, claims today that Serbia had a great opportunity to resolve the Kosovo issue together with extraditing Slobodan Milosevic to the Hague Tribunal. One of the leaders of DOS reveals that this exchange could have been arranged with George Bush Junior, who was at the time the new US President, but the President of the FRY at the time, Dr Vojislav Kostunica, immediately rejected that idea.

For me, a Serb from the USA, there was no difference in the rule or in the relation towards the Serbian people between the insidious communist Slobodan Milosevic and his wife Mira Markovic and the democrats gathered around the Democratic Opposition of Serbia, called DOS. What Sloba and Mira had done to the people, society, economy, and the country – ruined them, was just continued being done by democrats.

The Presidents Vojislav Kostunica and Boris Tadic

The DOS inherited clean and rich power. Serbian foreign debts were forgiven and, instead of searching for investors for the economic development, democrats started taking new loans, performing criminal company privatizations, and bringing foreign banks. They sought the money taken outside the country, but they never reported finding any of it. The DOS leaders started acquiring personal wealth. They continued the economy of destruction and the destroying of Serbia.

During the time of Tito, the US capital was brought into Serbia through the largest companies *Westinghouse* and *Boing*. I brought to Milosevic the KPMG, the greatest investment company from Washington. He first accepted it, and then rejected it, as well as its project for the Serbian transition. During the time of Zoran Ðinđic, I brought the representatives of the *City Bank* to Serbia, but the Serbian Prime Minister didn't even want to hear about it until 50,000 dollars were paid onto his personal bank account.

I will try to explain that by using one parallel. Mlađan Dinkic, an oppositionist and later a minister, wrote a book entitled *Economic Destructions*, in which he described how Milosevic had destroyed Serbian economy with criminalization and inflation. Upon that, the same Dinkic, in a quite similar manner, with economic destruction, destroyed the rest of the Serbian economy and its entire banking.

Mira Markovic, for example, ruined a reputable and strong textile industry of Yugoslavia by bringing into Serbia 30,000 Chinese, who were selling cheap Chinese and Turkish clothes on the streets and lea markets. Democrats, for example, ruined the pharmaceutical industry with criminal privatization. Drug factories were sold for 3.5 to 16.8 million euros, while their export was worth around 600 million euros. The renowned and credible Serbian banks were privatized by being replaced by surrogate banks with franchises of well-known world houses, which took over the financial market in Serbia with private and legal clients. Around five thousand workers were ired from Serbian banks, which weren't closed, but they don't work.

Democrats developed gray economy and corruption to that extent that a million of buildings were made in Serbia without municipal and building permits, and without any taxes paid for that illegal property. In order to solve that problem, Democrats suggested that the legalization of those criminal buildings gets free of charge?! The issue of illegal construction hasn't still been resolved. Serbia is the only country in the world that has more illegal than legal buildings. The experts have established that, in our country, the number of illegally constructed buildings has increased from 1.6 to 5 million. And, there are 4.5 million legally constructed buildings recorded in the cadastre.

Great foreign companies from the West do not easily decide to invest in Serbia, due to the corruption within the state systems. And, without the strong economy and the development of the industry, we cannot go any further. Democrats reduced Serbia to Belgrade, where there is developing economy, while other parts of the country languish economically or deteriorate. Seven hundred villages in Serbia are becoming desolate.

Politically, the new DOS leadership functioned according to Milosevic's war principle. A bit autistic President of the FRY, Dr Vojislav Kostunica shied away from the Americans, the IMF, World Bank, and International Community and put Serbia in a ghetto. They didn't even try to resolve the issue of Kosovo and Metohija, because Đinđic, Kostunica, and then Tadic, as well, were leading bad international politics and Serbia had bad relations with the world.

It is only today, three decades after Slobodan Milosevic came to power in Serbia and eighteen years after the Democrats came to power, that the citizens of Serbia place their former rulers in their right historical place. The public survey, conducted in the summer of 2018 in order to establish who the Serbs would vote for at the elections where some historical figures would participate, showed that Slobodan Milosevic was the greatest loser. In that survey, Tito was the most popular with 24.6%, Aleksandar Vucic was the second with 23.5%, Zoran Đinđic the third with 10.7%, and Slobodan Milosevic the last with just 7.4%. The young Serbs gave just 2.8% to Milosevic, while he was most supported by the elderly, aged over 60, with 10%. After Milosevic, the worst leaders were Kostunica with just 1.2% and Boris Tadic with 4%. That says it all about the authority of these persons after the destruction of Serbia.

At the beginning of 21st century, while Democrats were on power, the fifth and the most dangerous influence of the USA and the CIA was performed over Serbia. We can call it a period of the international killing of the Serbs and the installation of the US model of democracy. The period started in June 2001 with the extradition of Slobodan Milosevic to the Hague Tribunal for War Crimes. It continued by the exodus of the Serbs from Kosovo and Metohija in March 2007 and the declaration of the so-called independent country, Kosovo. It further moved on to the breaking up of the State Union of Serbia and Montenegro – it is now publicly said that Montenegro received 55 million dollars for abandoning Milosevic – and then to the offering of the democratic hand for the entrance of Serbia into the European Union, at the end of 2009. But, with one, still unclear, condition – with or without Kosmet as a part of Serbia.

Although the Republican George Bush Junior replaced the Democrat Bill Clinton on the position of the US President on 20th January 2001, the US foreign politics towards the official Belgrade didn't change. During his two terms of office, Bush continued tearing Serbia apart, because the officials from Belgrade couldn't persuade him that our country was important for the national security of the USA in the Balkans. Kostunica treated the USA as an enemy of the state.

The new Serbian President, Boris Tadic, missed the most opportunities to reform the country and to position it better in the region, Europe, and the world. Seemingly, he had good relations with Washington, but without any effects to Serbia. The same as Đinđic and Kostunica, Tadic also didn't deal much with the Kosovo issue. Tadic and his Democratic Party had enough time and absolute influence on the political and economic events in Serbia to improve the position of our country in every sense, but they wasted that historic opportunity.

For Barack Obama, the President who was seated in the White House from 2009 to 2017, Serbia was of no relevance. He let the European Union politically and economically exhaust us.

The incumbent US President Donald Trump, who has been surrounded by Slavs in his family for decades, has understanding for the Serbs and shows the readiness to support us in all the resolutions that we offer for the rising of Serbia and solving of the Kosovo and Metohija issue.

Ronald Reagan, the President of the party Dr Borko Djordjevic is a member of

HAND THE SERBS OVER

In the winter of 2004, from confidential sources of the Republican Party and the US Congress, I learned that the USA was getting ready to re-impose sanctions to my country. They had first been introduced by the Resolution of the UN Security Council on 30th May 1992 because of Serbia interfering in the internal issues of Bosnia and Herzegovina, and lifted on 2nd October 1996, after free multi-party elections in Bosnia without any outside interference. During the time of the embargo, Serbia and its people experienced the chaos caused by the black market, smuggling, and other forms of criminalized economy.

Eight years later, due to the failure to meet the international obligations of Serbia towards the Hague Tribunal, i.e. the extradition of Radovan Karadzic and General Ratko Mladic, the US Congress threatened to impose the US sanctions on the State Union of Serbia and Montenegro starting from 20th January 2005. As I was informed, the EU member states would join this embargo. Such measures would make the international position of the State Union of Serbia and Montenegro even more difficult and set back its economy. And, the consequence of that would be the further decline of the living standard of the people and deepening of their political agony.

I felt obliged to do something in order to prevent the introduction of international sanctions. I shared my concerns with a few American Serbs from California, who suggested that it was the best to send an open letter to Boris Tadic, the President of Serbia, and Vojislav Kostunica, the Prime Minister, and tell them to get in direct touch with Radovan Karadzic and Ratko Mladic and to persuade them to surrender and that we, the former US President Jimmy Carter and I, as intermediaries between the state and these Hague indictees and fugitives would "get in touch with Karadzic and Mladic and provide all conditions for their fair trial, not in the Hague, but in Belgrade".

The open letter composed by the Initiative Group of US Serbs from California and signed by me, told the President and the Prime Minister of Serbia, in the winter of 2004 that Jimmy Carter and I "have already been in touch with the US Ambassador for War Crimes Pierre-Richard Prosper". He "told us about the consent of the US government to put on the disposal of indictees all legal documentation and to provide them legal protection of the world's best lawyers, as well as to explore the possibility to be prosecuted by the Hague Tribunal in Belgrade".

The third man in the White House responsible for dangerous Serbs, Ambassador Pierre Prosper understood my proposals and advised me to make them official as the request of the Serbian people and country. Prosper was in charge of the Hague Tribunal on the behalf of the USA. When they arrived in the USA, the Minister of Diaspora Dr Vojislav Vukcevic and his assistant Vukman Krivokuća supported my proposal and agreed to transfer it to Boris Tadic and Vojislav Kostunica in the form of an open letter. Ambassador Prosper then accepted a conference phone call in which at least ten people participated. We asked him:

"Is the USA for or against this proposal that Karadzic and Mladic surrender to Belgrade authorities and that they get prosecuted in Serbia?"

"The USA isn't against it," replied Ambassador Prosper. "We won't veto it. And, who are you going to organize that with?"

"With Tadic and Kostunica," the Minister Vojislav Vukcevic replied to him.

"Good luck with that! Both of them are distrustful and do not keep their words," said Prosper and hung up.

This entire protocol was supposed to be made official and, therefore, we sent the open letter to the President and Prime Minister of Serbia and published it in the media. The Minister of Diaspora, Vukcevic, took the original letter, the complete proposal, and the plan of this mission, as well as the transcript of the conversation with Ambassador Pierre-Richard Prosper, to hand them over to Boris Tadic and Vojislav Kostunica. My intention was to save Karadzic and Mladic the humiliation and to save the Serbian people the shame they would feel if their brave representatives were treated as convicts without the right to tell the truth on their fight for freedom. The USA, the UN, the EU, and the entire Western world were turned against the Serbian people. As many as eighty of our people were indicted and declared criminals of war.

The list of most dangerous Serbs in the world included: Zeljko Raznatovic, Dr Vojislav Seselj, Slobodan Milosevic, Radovan Karadzic, and General Ratko Mladic. Then, in 2004, Arkan had already been dead, Voja Seselj had handed himself to the Hague Tribunal, Milosevic had been extradited to the Hague by the new democratic government of the Prime Minister Zoran Đinđic, and Karadzic and Mladic were on the run. Jimmy Carter, who met Radovan and Ratko in Pale in 1994, and whose wife, Rosalynn, found them so charming that she offered to take them to the Olympics in Atlanta in 1996, supported my proposal and agreed to join the action of extraditing Karadzic and Mladic.

I considered that Radovan Karadzic needed to hand himself in, in order to tell the truth to the Tribunal on the ight and calamities of the Serbian people in Bosnia and Herzegovina. If he got caught as a fugitive, he would become a man without human rights and a prisoner, but if he handed himself in, he would enjoy all human rights in the Hague, he would be a Serbian hero, and a fighter for the truth on the Serbs. At that point, the work and the life of Radovan Karadzic belonged more to the Serbian people than to his family. The question of the fate of Radovan Karadzic was, in my opinion, a national issue of the Serbs and the Serbian countries. In addition, Karadzic and his family members were in a great danger of the Americans and the Prosecutor's Of ice of the Hague Tribunal. The SFOR and EUFOR searched the houses and lats of Ljiljana, Aleksandar, and Sonja Karadzic over a dozen times, because they were suspected of not only cooperating with Radovan, but communicating with him, as well. The CIA specialists even confiscated several intimate possessions of Ljiljana and Sonja Karadzic in order to send them to forensic analysis, which was supposed to reveal a recent presence of Radovan Karadzic in his home or in the apartment of his daughter in Pale.

The USA announced a bounty of five million dollars to the person that reports or finds Radovan Karadzic. The USA spent around three million dollars a year looking for Radovan Karadzic. If Radovan surrendered, that budget would be re-allocated. The fact is, after the change of power in the White House, in 2001, when Bill Clinton was replaced by President George Bush Junior, he declared null and void the agreement between Radovan Karadzic and Ambassador Richard Holbrooke on non-attacking and the peaceful life of the leader of the Bosnian Serbs. The US hunt after Karadzic and Mladic started, as well as the pressure on the official Belgrade to extradite them to the Hague Tribunal as soon as possible. The refusal of that US request by Serbia was considered in Washington a "Serbian disrespect of international community, failure to fulfill its state obligations and disruption of good relations with the USA". Therefore, the Americans accepted my initiative, but on condition that the Belgrade government, i.e. Boris Tadic and Vojislav Kostunica, authorize me to be the Plenipotentiary Representative of the State Union of Serbia and Montenegro in the mission of voluntary surrendering of Karadzic and Mladic. Larry Burns, the special advisor of Ambassador Pierre-Richard Prosper, wrote the authorization which was supposed to be signed by the officials of the State Union of Serbia and Montenegro, as the only international subject, but also by the representatives of the Government of Serbia, which was the only one that could provide the guarantees to the accused Karadzic.

Radovan wasn't supposed to surrender to the authorities of the Republic of Srpska, because that country wasn't internationally recognized and wasn't able to use international political and legal institutions for negotiations and for the prosecution of the former president of the Republic of Srpska. Radovan Karadzic, while he was the president of the Serbian country within Bosnia and Herzegovina didn't have the possibility to complete the creation of the Republic of Srpska. Americans and Slobodan Milosevic forbade him to come to Dayton and to make the creation of the Republic of Srpska official during November 1995.

And, while I was expecting the answer of Boris Tadic and Vojislav Kostunica and phoning the Minister of Diaspora Dr Vojislav Vucevic on daily basis, some politicians appeared trying to refute my idea of obtaining the authorization for representing the country in this mission. Aleksandar Simic, an Advisor of the Prime Minister of Serbia for legal issues, said to a Belgrade daily *Blic* that according to the Constitution, the authorizations to an official negotiator can be given only by the Government of Serbia and, possibly, by the Council of Ministers of the State Union of Serbia and Montenegro, and that the President of Serbia didn't have such powers.

However, the Minister of Justice, Zoran Stojkovic said for the same daily *Blic* that "negotiation authorizations can be provided only by the State Union of Serbia and Montenegro, i.e. the Council for the Cooperation with the Hague Tribunal".

They hadn't read the open letter to Tadic and Kostunica and the claim in it stating that "involving Professor Dr Borko Djordjevic in this process implies that he obtains the status of the plenipotentiary negotiator and that the US State Department, at the request of the State Union of Serbia and Montenegro, issues him a consent to that, bearing in mind that he, apart from the citizenship of the State Union of Serbia and Montenegro, also has the citizenship of the USA" and, therefore, they didn't comment on it. They just declared Serbia incompetent to issue me the negotiating authorization.

Waiting to hear what President Tadic and the Prime Minister Kostunica thought about the matter, I was making plans with Jimmy Carter to involve Carter's Center from Atlanta in this project, as well as some influential US Congressmen and Senators, the politician Henry Kissinger, Joyce Neu, the Director of "Joan B. Kroc" Institute for Peace and Justice, the judge Richard Goldstone, a former public prosecutor of the Hague Tribunal, and also one of the world best known lawyers, Alan Dershowitz.

Karadzic already had three lawyers in the USA that had proved in 1996 that Radovan wasn't guilty of the charges he had been prosecuted for, both in the USA and in the Hague Tribunal. It was also envisaged that Karadzic and Mladic get tried in Belgrade by the five-member Trial Chamber, of which the four judges would be from Serbia and the Presiding Trial Judge from the EU. Under these terms, if he had handed himself in voluntarily, Radovan Karadzic would have been on pretrial release.

Borko Djordjevic and Jimmy Carter with his inscription

The reactions to my proposal in the Republic of Srpska and in Serbia were mostly encouraging and positive. Almost all the political parties in the Republic of Srpska welcomed the surrender of Karadzic, while SDS refrained from any comments because, as it was officially announced by this party, "it is inappropriate and impertinent to disturb the family that has had such problems as the Karadzic family".

Most citizens of the Republic of Srpska, if we could believe their media, considered that Radovan Karadzic was supposed to hand himself in. That was also the stand of Ostoja Barasin, a military and political analyst from Banja Luka and a former member of the cabinet of the President of the Republic of Srpska. David Leakey, the EUFOR Commander and Steven Schook, the Commander of the NATO headquarters in Sarajevo approved my proposal. They insisted on the surrender of Radovan Karadzic and Ratko Mladic:

"We will continue aggressively searching for the persons accused of war crimes and we expect the surrender of Karadzic and Mladic for two convincing reasons: first, for the benefit of their family and secondly, for the benefit of Bosnia and Herzegovina."

In Serbia, we had a full support of the Ministry of Diaspora of the Government of Serbia and of almost all Serbian media.

"I'm completely familiar with the initiative and I support it. I consider it to be quite serious. That is the only and the best solution for the Serbs. Besides, the initiator of the idea, Dr Borko Djordjevic, has already obtained the enormous trust of the leading representatives of Serbs in Bosnia and Herzegovina and Radovan Karadzic in the first place, which can be seen from the letters and correspondence of Dr Borko with Karadzic proving their familiarity and closeness. Djordjevic got acquainted with Karadzic and Mladic during the last war, when he, being as a medical doctor, helped the wounded. In the mid-1990s, he was in the negotiating mission in Bosnia together with Carter. Karadzic was rather satisfied with that mission," stated the Minister of Diaspora, Vojislav Vukcevic, while he was at an international conference in Budapest.

That initiative of mine was rejected because the Serbian rulers were running away from Radovan Karadzic and Ratko Mladic and, in that manner, rejecting their personal connection with the historical events and calamities of the Serbian people caused by their predecessor Slobodan Milosevic. Karadzic and Mladic surrendered to the Serbian authorities only when that suited the President of Serbia in order to gain some political points with the Americans and the EU. The creator of the Republic of Srpska and the Commander of the Serbian Army in Bosnia are still being tried in the Hague Tribunal. None of the politicians from Serbia and the Republic of Srpska takes any interest in them anymore.

LAWSUITS AGAINST MIRA, MARKO, AND MARIJA

President Donald Trump has, to some extent, changed the attitude of Washington towards Serbia and, by that, he has distanced himself from the war politics of the USA in the 1990s, led by the US Presidents George Bush Senior and Bill Clinton. Rejecting their political heritage, which tarnished the reputation of the USA in the world, President Trump has opened the door for a dialogue with Serbia. Trump is offering us the possibility to make an agreement with the Albanians regarding Kosovo and Metohija, indicating that the USA would respect such an agreement. We should use this chance given by the official Washington.

The Serbs and Serbia should file a lawsuit against the former government of the USA and the former presidents George Bush and Bill Clinton for their seizing of Serbian private and state property in Kosmet and for it to be returned to the Serbs. Such lawsuits have been filed against the State Department and the US residents and they had positive outcomes - the return of the property to the states of Panama and Iran, which had been taken with the concordance and in the jurisdiction of the USA.

In the fall of 2018, the first lawsuits of Serbian citizens suffering from cancer were announced against the NATO for having dropped uranium bombs on us. In Nis, the Council was formed for the preparation of a lawsuit against the twelve countries that participated in the bombardment of Serbia in 1999. This lawsuit is supported by Russia and Israel. Professor Solomon Budnik, the President of the Public Tribunal and Arbitrage International in Tel Aviv, suggested to a law of ice Aleksic from Nis that this court should be the arbitrage in the case against the countries participating in the NATO aggression.

The NATO bombs in Serbia conducted an ecocide. The depleted uranium from the NATO bombs and the poison from the destroyed factories and chemical facilities entered the air, water, soil, and the food chain. That is why malignant diseases are three times more frequent here than in the world. In Serbia, in every 100,000 citizens, there are 5,500 cancer patients registered, while that number is 2,000 in the world! Since 2002, the mortality just due to leukemia has increased by 139%. The number of cancer patients increases by 2% annually in Serbia, while in the world, it grows by 0.6%. We mustn't leave to the young generations the destroyed country and the problems we can't talk about, and for which we can't sue the villains that created them. We must sue all those that, together with Slobodan Milosevic, destroyed Serbia and Kosmet. By that, I mean the members of Slobodan Milosevic's family as well, his wife Mira Markovic, his son Marko Milosevic, and his daughter Marija Milosevic. They got rich in Serbia, ran away from it, and they now have a happy and wealthy life abroad. They left us the impoverished and demolished Serbia and they led into the world with Serbian treasure and money.

Mira Markovic escaped to Russia in 2005 and got political asylum there. In Serbia, she has been accused of committing illegal actions. The Interpol has issued a warrant after her, but the Russian police refuse to arrest her, probably because of her strong connections in Russia. During the '90s, while she was still ruling in Serbia, she was a regular member of the Russian Academy of Social Sciences and a visiting professor of the Lomonosov Moscow State University.

How Slobodan Milosevic, Mira Markovic, and their children ruled

We will probably never ind out how she can afford so many years of her exile in the elite Moscow settlement Barvikha, how large her wealth exactly is, and, most importantly, how she acquired it. Because, not even the houses in Pozarevac, the sold house in Tolstojeva Street, the lat of her daughter Marija, confiscated due to the debts of her business partner, and all the real estate that Marko Milosevic had in Belgrade and Pozarevac would be enough to provide the life in that settlement –one of the most expensive in the world.

Officially, Mirjana Markovic receives just her pension of less than 60,000 RSD. Today, media report that, allegedly, before she escaped, Mira Markovic had taken from Villa *Mir* the artwork and a part of the treasure of Jovanka Broz. Thus, it is still unknown what happened to the two oil paintings by Paja Jovanovic *The Dance* and *The Country Party,* seven sculptures by Frano Krsinic and two by Mestrovic, *Njegos* and Melody, three oil paintings by Milan Konjovic, four landscapes by Petar Lubarda, and *Lepoglava* by Mosa Pijade. The others missing are: *Landscape with Pine Forest* by Nadezda Petrovic, *Recess* by Ljuba Ivanovic, *Sunny Landscape* by Milo Milutinovic, as well as the sculptures by Petar Pallavicini, Frano Krsinic, Oto Logo, but also numerous works by foreign authors: *Return from the Market* by an unknown Flemish artist, around twenty paintings of Dutch, French, Russian, Roman, and Viennese origin dating from 17th, 18th, and 19th century. I heard some information that she had taken diamonds out of Serbia, the ones that had been bought for her during the time of her ruling over Serbia.

According to the verdict of the Higher Court in Belgrade in the process against the former Director of the Directorate of the Yugoslav Left, the wife of Slobodan Milosevic, Dr Mira Markovic was sentenced to one year in jail for the abuse of her authority by allocating a state-owned apartment to her secretary and the nanny of her son.

As media reported, her and Sloba's son, Marko Milosevic, had been engaged in the trade with cigarettes, oil, and foreign exchange in Serbia,. He owned a club *Madona*, a company *Bambilend* in Pozarevac, and a bakery chain. After the 5th October 2000 and the change of government, he moved to Russia. He was accused of coercion in the Municipal Court of Pozarevac. He was on the run and he was wanted by the Interpol. In Russia and Belarus, he owns companies and has a new family. He lives in Moscow.

Marija Milosevic fled to Montenegro. It has been reported that she first lived in Niksic and, then, in Cetinje. She was married to Slobodan Bulatovic, a tourist inspector from Cetinje. In Belgrade, she owned the radio station *Kosava* and a villa in Dedinje. In Serbia, she is wanted for a trial for unauthorized possession of weapons and shooting at the officers during the arrest of her father on 1st April 2001. Marija is also on the Serbian police's wanted list.

A lawsuit should be filed at the International Court of Justice and at Serbian courts against Mira Markovic, Marko Milosevic, and Marija Milosevic for wresting Serbian property and capital, with the request to return to Belgrade the money and treasure they have taken from Serbia. These three lawsuits are not just the matter of national justice, but of Serbian dignity, as well, which needs to be restored, and, in that manner, the reputation of the Serbian people in the world will also be improved.

EPILOGUE

The state politics of Serbia has been directed against the interests of the Serbian people and its own citizens for almost thirty years now. The political heritage of Slobodan Milosevic and DOS is a complicated and heavy burden. The new President of Serbia, Aleksandar Vucic, demonstrates with his political actions, as a statesman, that he represents the public interests of citizens. On behalf of the people and citizens, he negotiates with the Albanians from Kosmet and the EU and USA officials and makes decisions that are in the best interest of Serbia.

Aleksandar Vucic has accomplished to have the leading position in those negotiations and he has created the situation in which he can publicly fight for the Serbian national interest. And, to my mind, that is primarily to return Kosovo and Metohija to be a part of Serbia, as envisaged by the Constitution of the Republic of Serbia. Secondly, it is for Serbia to become an equal member of the European Union. Thirdly, it is for it to remain militarily neutral. And, fourthly, to become a modern country.

The President is faced with the reality in which he needs to correct the blunders of his predecessors. The socalled independent Kosovo is a fake country, which cannot exist in reality, because it functions as a stolen Serbian land. The infrastructure in Kosovo is stolen from Serbia –traffic, water supply, sewage system, electricity, landline and mobile telephony, companies... Kosovo, governed by terrorists and mobsters, is a dangerous country which isn't in the best interest of the USA and which can jeopardize the stability of Europe.

That is a trap that Vucic needs to beware, because there is a danger that Albanian leaders blame him for the bad situation in Kosmet and for the refusal of the possibility for progress of the so-called independent Kosovo. In order to avoid that trap, the Americans need to be explained in a diplomatic manner that Kosovo was the worst political investment of the former presidents Bill Clinton and George Bush and that this Kosovo today is the country without any future.

The US President Donald Trump

President Donald Trump doesn't want to continue implementing the warmongering politics of Clinton and Bush. The Americans understand Serbs and support us. We need to propose to Washington to withdraw the decision of the US administration on the recognition of the so-called independent Kosovo. There is a formula for initiating that process. That is a Serbian lawsuit against the former US Government and Presidents Clinton and Bush for wresting Serbian private and state property in Kosmet and for it to be returned to Serbs.

The same as the United States understand and support Montenegro, they can understand and support Serbia. The official Podgorica, which supports Aleksandar Vucic, can help Serbia raise its reputation in the world and join the EU.

ABOUT THE AUTHOR

Borko Djordjevic, a renowned plastic surgeon, was born in Pirot, Serbia. He completed his education in Pirot, Belgrade, Livingstone, Montclair, Philadelphia, and Columbus. However, he spent his youth in Belgrade and he feels this city as a part of his own being. He tries to spend most of his time in it, as much as his business activities around the world allow him. He lives and works on the route Belgrade-Igalo-Dubai-Palm Springs, California, where he has surgeries.

He graduated from the Faculty of Medicine in Belgrade within the deadline and, as a young and promising physician, he desired to specialize in gynecology. However, injustice has accompanied him from his early age. In quite usual circumstances at the time, when virtues and skills weren't much appreciated, the right to that specialization was assigned to a different person of the opposite sex. The one who was making decisions knew what they needed, but that certainly wasn't something beneficial to the, at the time, socialist society, but to them personally.

What kind of gynecologist Borko Djordjevic would have been will remain a mystery, but that he is a magnificent plastic surgeon can be best illustrated by the *BBC* which classifies him among the ten all-time best plastic surgeons in the world. His work speaks best. It's not a coincidence that he was asked to make doubles of Saddam Hussein. Apart from that, he also made doubles of Elvis Presley, as well as of many other world stars, such as Larry King, Sir Elton John, Joan Collins, the Gabor sisters, and of other persons from the sport and public life.

As a prominent doctor in his field for many years, Dr Borko B. Djordjevic has always been at the forefront of the latest achievements of cosmetic and reconstructive surgery. Having the certificate of the *American Board of Plastic and Reconstructive Surgery* and being a member of the *American Academy of Cosmetic Surgery* (AACS), Dr Borko B. Djordjevic MD, specialized in General Plastic Surgery, as well as Esthetic and Reconstructive Surgery, including face-lifting, rhinoplasty, blepharoplasty, chemical peeling, augmentation and reduction of breasts, arms and legs, reduction and transformation of the hips and abdomen, liposuction, and correction and reconstruction of the genitals.

Dr Borko Djordjevic MD has worked as the Head of Residents in Plastic and Reconstructive Surgery, Hand, Genital and Cosmetic Surgery at the *Riverside Methodist Hospital* in Columbus, Ohio. He continued his education at prestigious institutions, such as Stanford and Northwestern University. Dedicated to learning new techniques, he has participated in International Symposia with some of the supreme world surgeons. His works have been published in numerous books and medical journals.

Dr Borko B. Djordjevic MD has worked as an assistant professor for the subject Plastic and Reconstructive Surgery at the Faculty of Medicine, the University of Belgrade. He has been a corresponding editor of the faculty's *Journal for Medical Researches* and the manager of the *Cosmetic Surgery Fellowship Training Program.*

In Yugoslavia, he was a Communist, in the USA, a Republican with a high function in California. In the 1990s, as a patriot, he participated in a peace mission in Serbia, Montenegro, and Bosnia and Herzegovina. He cooperated with Slobodan Milosevic, Dr Radovan Karadzic, Jimmy Carter, Ronald Reagan, and George Bush. In 1994, he received the special authorization by the former US President Jimmy Carter to assist Carter's Center in Atlanta, Georgia, in its efforts to reach peace in Bosnia and Yugoslavia and he was personally meritorious for the arrival of President Carter in Bosnia.

He is the author of the book *The Glass Peace* about Carter's peace in Bosnia and Herzegovina in 1994 and about his life in the USA. For this book, he was awarded the Charter of the Centre of Emigrants of Serbia.

Today, Mr. Djordjevic, as a member of the US Republican Party and a Serbian citizen, has an initiative to expand the cooperation with President Donald Trump and the new US Administration.

DOKUMENTA

US newspapers write about Dr. Borko Djordjevic as a leader among the Republican Doctors of Medicine

239

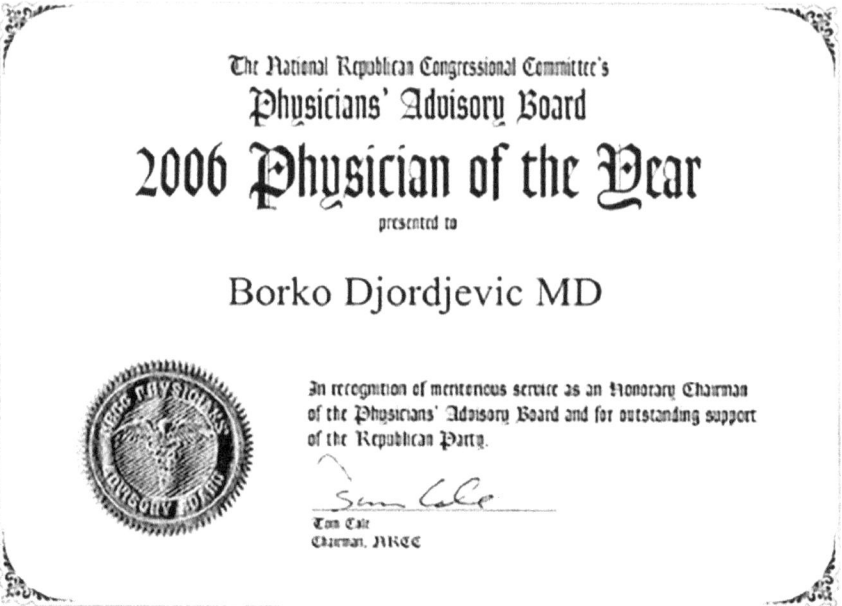

Dr. Borko Djordjevic was declared the US Physician of the Year in 2006

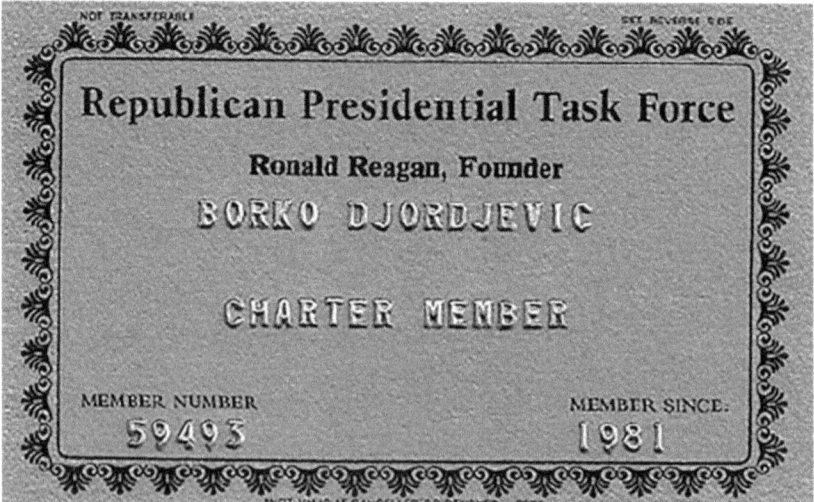

Party membership card of Dr. Borko Djordjevic, the USA

TO: Dr. Borko B. Djordjevic   DATE: 12/17/03

FROM: Congressman Tom Reynolds, Chairman   NOTES: Call us as soon as you

RE: See Below   Received this fax —

    Congratulations! Tom

    1-866-897-2974

Let me begin by saying CONGRATULATIONS! As Chairman of the National Republican Congressional Committee, it is my pleasure to inform you that you have been nominated for:

The Physicians' Advisory Board's
PHYSICIAN OF THE YEAR AWARD
Representing California

Dr. Djordjevic, THIS IS QUITE AN HONOR! The Physician of the Year Award will be presented to our physicians who have been instrumental in helping **pass the largest tax cut in a generation keeping the White House and Congress in Republican hands and providing the leadership and input to improve the healthcare system in America!**

Our recipients will be selected in January and the awards presentation will take place in early 2004 in Washington, D.C. during our **Annual Board Meeting**. Based on your contributions---both personally and economically during 2003---I feel confident Dr. Djordjevic that you will be selected to receive this prestigious award.

This should be great for your practice!

We are also marking this occasion by publishing the recipients' names in a full page **Wall Street Journal** ad---I've included a mock-up of the ad for your review. Please proof the ad and confirm the spelling of your name as you would like it to appear. I'd ask that you call my assistant Bonnie Martin at 1-866-897-2974 in the next 48 hours with your approval. **We want** the ad all set to go the day the recipients are announced.

Congratulations again! Please call Bonnie right away at 1-866-897-2974 with your approval.

Tom Reynolds

Paid for by the National Republican Congressional Committee and not authorized by any candidate or candidate's committee.
www.nrcc.org

The Annual Award presented to Dr. Borko Djordjevic for his activities in the Health Committee of the Republican Party

THE
REPUBLICAN SENATORIAL

MEDAL OF FREEDOM

*"The highest honor
the Republican members
of the U.S. Senate
can bestow."*

The Medal of Freedom bestowed to Dr. Borko Djordjevic

REPUBLICAN SENATORIAL

———————— MEDAL OF FREEDOM ————————

NRSC Chairman
Senator Bill Frist, M.D.

Inner Circle Chairman
Senator Sam Brownback

Medal of Freedom Recipients
Ronald Reagan
Margaret Thatcher
H. Norman Schwarzkopf

February 27, 2002

Borko Djordjevic, MD
1091 N Palm Canyon Dr.
Palm Springs, CA 92262

Dear Dr. Djordjevic:

The Republican Senatorial Medal of Freedom is the highest honor the Republican Members of the United States Senate can bestow upon an individual. This prestigious award is presented to those extraordinary individuals who have shown a lifelong commitment to preserving the conservative principles that are the foundation of the Republican Party and the lifeblood of our country.

This high honor has been endowed upon our nation's and our world's greatest defenders of liberty, economic freedom and military strength.

As you can see from the enclosed flyer, previous recipients include former President Ronald Reagan, former British Prime Minister Margaret Thatcher and Retired General Norman Schwarzkopf.

I write to you today to announce your unanimous nomination to receive the Republican Senatorial Medal of Freedom.

The Medal of Freedom awarded by the US Republican Party

Republican Senatorial Medal of Freedom
Certificate of Commendation

Presented to

Borko Djordjevic, MD

Recipient of the
Republican Senatorial Medal of Freedom
Two thousand and two

As Nominated By:

Senator Bill Frist, M.D.

The Medal of Freedom, the Certi icate on Commendation presented to Dr.
Borko Djordjevic in 2002

244

INTERNATIONAL COLLEGE OF SURGEONS
A World Federation of General Surgeons and Surgical Specialists, Inc.
United States Section

1995-96
EXECUTIVE COMMITTEE:

President
Said A. Daee, M.D.
Grombelt, MO

President-Elect
Raymond A. Dieter, Jr., M.D.
Glen Ellyn, IL

Immediate Past President
Jalal Afnan, M.D.
Cleveland, OH

Secretary
John C. Scott, M.D.
Seattle, Washington

Treasurer
John B. Chang, M.D.
Roslyn, NY

Chairman, Board of Regents
Kazem Fathie, M.D.
Las Vegas, NV

Specialty Groups Representative
Neil L. Simstein, M.D.
Winston-Salem, NC

HONORARY FELLOWS:

Nicholas S. Assali, M.D.
Hugh R. K. Barber, M.D.
Ralph C. Benson, M.D.
Denton A. Cooley, M.D.
Robert J. Corry, M.D.
Donald L. Custis, M.D.
Michael E. DeBakey, M.D.
Virgil T. DeVault, M.D.
Tomlinson Fort, M.D.
Joseph G. Fortner, M.D.
C. Richard A. Gilbert, M.D.
William Goldman, M.D.
Alfred N. Goldsmith, M.D.
Lazar J. Greenfield, M.D.
George J. Hayes, M.D.
Robert E. Hermann, M.D.
Robert A. Hingson, M.D.
Howard P. House, M.D.
Miles H. Irving, M.D.
Georgeanna Seeger Jones, M.D.
Howard W. Jones, M.D.
Jerome B. Kaufman, M.D.
Harold E. Kleinhert, M.D.
Henry P. Leis, Jr., M.D.
Anthony J. Maniglia, M.D.
Homer F. Marsh, M.D.
Franklin D. Murphy, M.D.
Oliver K. Niess, M.D.
Wesley W. Parke, M.D.
Col. Basil A. Pruitt, Jr., M.D.
Robert D. Ray, M.D.
Victor Richards, M.D.
Pedro A. Rubio, M.D.
Kurt Semm, M.D.
Jerry Mark Shuck, M.D.
Austin E. Smith, M.D.
Ralph Snyder, M.D.
Thomas Starzl, M.D.
Philip Thorek, M.D.
Malcolm C. Todd, M.D.
Donald D. Trunkey, M.D.
Hans von Leden, M.D.
Paul H. Ward, M.D.
Allen B. Weingold, M.D.
Edward R. Woodward, M.D.
George D. Zuidema, M.D.

December 6, 1996

David Djordjevic, MD
1091 N. Palm Canon
Palm Springs, CA 92262

Dear Doctor Djordjevic:

It is my pleasure to inform you that by vote of the International Executive Committee, you have been unanimously elected a New Fellow of the International College of Surgeons-US Section.

I feel confident that you will enjoy your relationships within our organization. ICS aims to serve as a catalyst in bringing together surgeons from all over the world to facilitate an international exchange of surgical knowledge and to foster friendship amongst its members.

On behalf of our officers and members, I extend to you our warmest welcome and I hope that you will choose to participate in our worldwide congresses, humanitarian activities, and educational programs. I also encourage you to get involved in the administrative business of the College at the National, Federation, and International levels.

Attached you will find information regarding the many benefits we offer. Also, I have included an application for membership which I would like you to pass along to a colleague. If you have any further questions, please feel free to call Chicago headquarters, Membership department at 1-(800)-766-FICS.

Congratulations and best personal regards to you.

Sincerely,

Said A. Daee, MD
President, ICS - US Section

1516 North Lake Shore Drive, Chicago, Illinois 60610-1694; Telephone (312) 787-6274; Facsimile (312) 787-9289
Founded in Geneva, Switzerland; Incorporated in Washington, DC

The International College of Surgeons informing Dr. Djordjevic that he has become their member

The National Republican Congressional Committee

2003 National Leadership Award

presented to:

Borko Djordjevic MD

Honorary Chairman
Physicians' Advisory Board

In recognition of outstanding service and commitment to Republican ideals, and in particular for assistance and guidance administered to the Republican Leadership in the area of Health Care Reform.

Tom De Lay

Congressman Tom DeLay
Majority Leader

National Republican Leadership Award for Dr. B. Djordjevic in 2006

OFFICIAL PAB RELEASE:

DR. BORKO B. DJORDJEVIC
APPOINTED TO
PHYSICIANS' ADVISORY BOARD

Washington, D.C. - Officials from the National Republican Congressional Committee announced that Dr. Borko B. Djordjevic has been appointed to serve on the Physicians' Advisory Board (PAB) in recognition of valuable contributions and dedication to the Republican Party.

Dr. Djordjevic will serve the state of California and is expected to play a crucial role in the Party's efforts to involve top physicians in the process of government reform.

The Physicians' Advisory Board is part of the National Republican Congressional Committee, and is dedicated to making sure that physicians have a voice in Washington.

Dr. Djordjevic, who has long supported Republican ideals, particularly healthcare reform, will be a key member of the Board.

Invitation for Dr. Djordjevic to be a member of the Physicians' Advisory Board of the US Republican Congressional Committee

Dr. Borko B. Djordjevic
SERBIAN INFERNO

Translated from Serbian by Jelena Ilic

Publisher
Dr. Borko B. Djordjevic

For the publisher
Marko Lopusina

Editor
Marko Lopusina

Technical editor
Nevenka Antic

Language editor/Proof-reader Dragana Zigic

Printed by
SZGR Jovan Antic, Belgrade

www.ingramcontent.com/pod-product-compliance
Lightning Source LLC
Chambersburg PA
CBHW051244020426

42333CB00025B/3041